# STREET FOOD REVOLUTION

# STREET FOOD REVOLUTION

Inspiring recipes
and stories from the
new food heroes

*Richard Johnson*

Photography by Laura Edwards

Kyle Books

I would like to thank Big Mike, Woogie, Eve and Michaela for making me the man I am today – which is to say Happy, with a Big, Loving Family. Thank you to Jess, for inspiring me to take this silly street food dream and make it a reality. And thank you to my darling Neris and Chops. They are the ones who stood, smiling, in the middle of Ludlow's Market Square with a sign saying British Street Food Awards This Way. For an entire weekend. And they are the ones who started having dreams about eating indoor food again one day – at a table. But never complained. I dedicate this book to them.

*Richard Johnson*

First published in Great Britain in 2011
by Kyle Books
23 Howland Street
London W1T 4AY
general.enquiries@kylebooks.com
www.kylebooks.com

ISBN 978-0-85783-000-5

Text © 2011 Richard Johnson
Book design © 2011 Jake Tilson Studio
Photography © 2011 Laura Edwards

Project editor: Jenny Wheatley
Designer: Jake Tilson Studio
Photographer: Laura Edwards
Typography: Trader names handwritten by
    Petra Barran; recipe titles made from an
    alphabet handwritten by Petra Barran
Recipe tester: Sue Ashworth
Food stylist: Joy Skipper
Props stylist: Krissy Hodgkinson
Editorial assistant: Estella Hung
Proofreader: Ruth Baldwin
Production: Nic Jones and Sheila Smith

Richard Johnson is hereby identified as the author of this work in accordance with Section 77 of the Copyright, Designs and Patents Act 1988.

A Cataloguing In Publication record for this title is available from the British Library.

Colour reproduction by Sang Choy in Singapore.
Printed in China by Toppan Leefung Printing Ltd.

# contents

# INTRODUCTION

It was Marco Pierre White who gave me the idea. It was a summer lunchtime – in a New York park – and we were hungover from a night of Sambuca at Jay-Z's party. Sat on the grass, and eating a street-vendor's burger slathered with ketchup, we wondered why we weren't offering the same thing in Britain. I decided, then and there, that I would do something about the state of British street food. Once I had ordered another burger.

In my time as a food writer and broadcaster I've travelled the world. And some of the best food I've ever eaten has been on the streets – whether it was the streets of Bethlehem, with its hole-in-the-wall falafel shacks serving up pittas fat with creamy hummus, pickle and broad beans, or the streets of Mandalay, with bowls of fishy noodles still salty from the sea. But coming back home to Britain was always a disappointment.

Our restaurant food was the envy of the world. But our street food? What a complete and utter embarrassment. It was either a bag of chips, a Mr Whippy,

or a sausage from a rusty metal handcart pushed along by a Polish man with three fingers. Clearly, we needed a revolution. And, like any good revolution, it had to start on the street. With the help of a full contacts book – and a Family Railcard – I set about seeing what was out there.

There was Tony, who ran Stoats Porridge Bars. He sold cranachan porridge, with Scottish raspberries, honey and cream, from a shiny silver truck on the Royal Mile in Edinburgh. There was Chris, who was a real aesthete. He sold the perfect burger from Rocket & Relish – a classic American Airstream trailer in Belfast. And there was George, who made fresh, crispy pastries on board the Churros Bros Citroën H van in London. Along with hundreds of others, they entered the British Street Food Awards.

At the finals, the judges were amazed at what they saw. The Polish man was clearly sharing the pavement with a new generation of street food heroes. They were all characters. Big mouths who had learnt to make their living on the streets. Men and women who wanted to be part of the food revolution that's happening in this country, but didn't necessarily have the capital they needed to open a restaurant. The results were staggering.

Judging by the crowds of people who came to Ludlow for the Awards, the people of Britain find the idea exciting. We aren't frightened of street food any more. We've been on holiday, we've seen street food markets for ourselves, and we realise that the people who stayed and ate in the hotel restaurant were just as likely to get food poisoning as the people who went out and ate something cooked on the street – right in front of our eyes.

Street food, in many ways, is better than restaurant food. For a start, it's cheap and fresh. Unlike a lot of restaurant food, which is expensive and left standing on a hot-plate until some sniffy waiter deigns to bring it to your table. So whether it's Dominic of Caffe Banba grinding just the beans he needs (so his coffee tastes alive rather than dead), Matt Timms of Greengages making his bread on site, or

Rich of Hall's Dorset Smokery actually smoking the fish in front of you, it's all as fresh as fresh can be. Street food is all about offering the kind of food that we want to eat. Restaurants are hung up on some received notion of what constitutes 'good food' – the street isn't the place for that kind of snobbery. And street food sellers buy local and seasonal as a matter of course because that's what's cheapest – margins are so tight there's often no choice.

The new generation of British mobilers have none of the grit, or the grease, which used to authenticate the whole street food experience. And their ingredients have improved. They take care about the provenance of their meat. Where you used to find limp white iceberg, you now find organic lamb's ear. And where once you squeezed on an (unidentified) red sauce, you now find a rich, homemade tomato ketchup. That's actually got tomatoes in it.

They say that our islands are too cold for street food. Rubbish. New York is hardly tropical, and it's the street food capital of the world. Korea gets snow in the winter, and there are street food sellers everywhere. Admittedly, a bit of warm weather wouldn't hurt. People would go out more, stay out more, and eat out more – the average Thai eats out 17 times a month. But I'm not complaining. There's nothing like a bag of hot chestnuts and a mug of hot chocolate on a cold winter's day.

Street food is all about doing one thing – and doing it well. Which is where it scores over restaurant fare. Ask a resident of Mumbai, and they'll tell you – with pride – that the city's restaurants are for tourists. They will recommend that you go and eat the food cooked by the blind chaatwala behind the railway station. Just over there. Beside the open drain. There's something about discovering authentic food that makes it so much tastier.

I will always remember the main square in Marrakesh where, at sundown, hundreds of stalls strung with different coloured lightbulbs started to cook. Sellers pulled on shirtsleeves, or sang 'God Save The Queen' – whatever it took to get your attention. And any table you chose was 'the best seat in the house'. Whether you ordered the braised sheep's head or the couscous with fresh mint, it all came with a dose of theatre.

Eat out of your comfort zone. You only live once. If you're in the Philippines and want to try the congealed pig's blood (known as Betamax because of its rectangular shape) or the chicken feet, you should head for the street food markets. And if you want to try balut or penoy – incubated duck eggs with or without a 16-to-18-day-old embryo – it's the street markets where you'll get lucky. If lucky is the right word.

The street food revolution is happening all across Europe. In Berlin it's rösti – huge, plate-sized portions of fried potato, slathered with apple sauce. And in Rome it's pizza. Although street pizza is very different from the pizzeria pizza. Unlike the 12-in rounds you find in a restaurant, pizza a taglio is made on large square trays, and sold by the rectangle. It's much easier to hold, and leaves you with one hand free to steer your Vespa.

We have a noble tradition of street food in Britain – as far back as the 12th century, shopkeepers sold hot sheep's feet. By the 18th century they were hawking pies and pasties, and by the 19th century it was everything from warm eels to pickled whelks, oysters, fried fish and hot peas. With a slice of rhubarb tart for dessert. Something, however, happened along the way. And we became prudish. By the end of the Victorian era, eating in public was considered suitable only for the working classes.

It took the burgeoning Farmers' Market movement to make street food popular again. Thanks to the markets, it became acceptable (and acceptably middle class)

to eat a sausage in a bun – if the sausage was rare breed and the bun was a hand-drawn sourdough. A new generation considered street food. And when they saw the exciting developments in America, they got very excited about the idea of high-quality meals on wheels.

Street food in America had struggled with working-class roots – it came from the 1970s 'roach coaches', which sold cheap food to Mexican workers. They migrated up the coast to LA – and east to New York. They fed the the janitors, the secretaries, and the guys on the construction sites. But then the food writers discovered them. All of a sudden, street food was for people in the know, who wanted something spontaneous – and authentic.

And, as it happened, cool. American street food had that element of theatre. The Elysburg lemon, for instance, sells the sweetest, sourest homemade lemonade. From a 10-ft fruit made of bright yellow polyurethane. And Maximum Minimus sells pulled pork sandwiches from a lunch wagon that's been transformed into a giant silver pig. It's got ears, a snout and a tail – and even a giant pair of sunglasses if it turns sunny. In America, street food is showbusiness.

Mobilers on both sides of the Atlantic now use social media. Facebook and Twitter are cheap and effective ways of telling people where you'll be trading, and what you'll be serving. Two minutes after tweeting, Alice Shin, of the LA food truck Kogi BBQ, was surrounded by zombies – like *The Night of the Living Dead*. 'I saw all these people walking out of buildings toward the truck,' she says, 'and they were all looking at their phones and BlackBerries. It was both cool and creepy.'

Restaurants feel slightly old hat by comparison. These days, we want a relaxed, free-wheeling dining experience. Which is why 'pop-up' restaurants (temporary restaurants in a space of somebody else's making) have been so successful. As have supper clubs, held in people's houses. We like the idea that the trappings of a dining room are negotiable. And we like the idea of eating somewhere and something that's

a little bit different. Which is where street food comes in.

Street food is revolutionising Britain's food culture forever. Gordon Ramsay claimed that we had a long way to go before we became a great culinary nation because food wasn't enjoyed from 'the bottom up' – well, street food is making that happen. It is colonising our high streets. It is reclaiming our public spaces. And it is showing us all that good food doesn't need to be stuck away in a Michelin restaurant with a menu no one can understand. To the barricades, comrades!

*Richard Johnson*

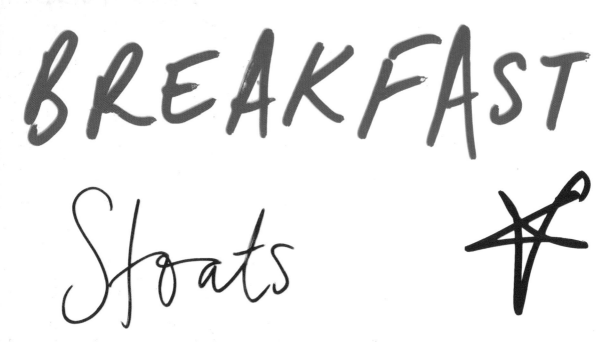

# BREAKFAST
## Stoats

Porridge is as Scottish as it gets. But — at the Stoats porridge trailer — they don't bang on about it. There's no bagpipe music playing in the background. And no stag's head on the wall. 'We thought about naming our porridge flavours after the clans,' says the trailer's owner, Tony Stone. 'But we decided against it. We resisted the temptation to turn up the Scottishness. The packaging has got "Made In Scotland" on it, but that's it. Our key message is "We're quirky and cool", not "We're from Scotland and we've got kilts on".'

Porridge oats grow well in these parts. They have a greater tolerance of rain than wheat, rye or barley — and don't need a long, hot summer. They are a superfood that lowers your cholesterol and reduces your blood pressure. They are gluten-free, low in calories, and low on the Glycaemic Index — which means that they release their energy slowly. The complex carbohydrates in a bowl of porridge help to balance the blood sugar levels and leave you feeling full up for longer. But let's be honest — porridge has a PR problem.

It's old-fashioned. It is shrouded in the dark, prehistoric mythology of the 'spurtle' — the carved wooden stick that's used to stir the porridge. According to tradition, you have to stir the porridge clockwise, because an anti-clockwise stir will invoke the Devil. You must then eat the porridge standing up, out of respect for the noble dish, or pour it into your 'porridge drawer' where, once it has cooled, you can cut it up into slices. Porridge isn't quirky and fashionable. Never has been. But, with Stoats, Tony Stone is giving it a go.

Tony serves up his porridge with a topping of thick, fruity jam from the Borders. Or honey and Balvenie whisky from Speyside. 'The whisky isn't heavy or harsh,' says Tony, 'and as soon as it hits the heat, the alcohol evaporates.' But the best seller is his porridge topped with tablet — a sweet Scottish fudge. It came about after the man at the Edinburgh farmers' market, where Stoats are based, offered Tony his offcuts. 'He said "I've got all of this left — try it." It melted over the top of the porridge. Molten almost. And then we stirred in a fistful of apples and grapes. Very, very good.'

# And then we stirred in a fistful of apples and grapes. Very, very good.

At the market, in the shadow of the castle, people are particular about their porridge. Which is why even the Stoats 'classic' comes in three different varieties: one with brown sugar and cream, one with milk, and one with water and salt. The water-and-salt version isn't a big seller in Edinburgh. 'Less than 5 per cent of our turnover,' says Tony. 'But in Glasgow, it's 20 per cent. And in Inverness it's 30 per cent. The further north you get, the more extreme the porridge. It's like, "We're proper Scots – we're hard. Porridge is part of our national identity." '

Tony came up with the idea for Stoats when he was operations manager of a hotel in Wales.

He was on his teabreak, and catching up on the news. But every paper he opened seemed to be telling the same story. 'I remember reading: "10 Reasons To Eat Porridge", "Madonna Eats Porridge" and "Porridge Sales Up By 81 per cent" in a single day. Porridge was everywhere. It got the old brain ticking over. It wasn't that I wanted to bring porridge to the people – I was just a businessman who saw a gap in the market.'

The story behind the Stoats name remains a mystery. Even to Tony. His second name is Stone. And 'Stoats' is Stone and oats put together. But he also liked the idea of having a St Oats day – to celebrate the patron saint of porridge. Plus

a 'stoater' in Scots is something of exceptional quality. 'If there are three reasons to go for a name, you've got to go for it,' says Tony. 'And Stoats is such a nice symmetrical word. Good for branding. It just seemed to stick. We still get one person a week going, "What's the difference between a stoat and a weasel?" But at least we're getting noticed.'

Tony and Bob, a friend from school, first conceived Stoats as a chain of porridge bars, where cool people would go for a bowl of something warming and a read of the day's newspapers. The porridge would be the best blend of Scottish organic oats, and served with a wide range of Tony's trademark toppings. 'But I only had a bit of money from a property sale in Wales, and a £4,000 loan from the Prince's Trust,' says Tony. 'Not the £400,000

that Bob and I needed. So we had to scale the idea back a bit.'

Which is an understatement – Tony and Bob bought a trailer. They went looking for something unusual, and found it on Catersell. It was the sort of hot-dog trailer you would expect to see parked up at a 1970s American baseball game. 'Bob and I didn't want a bog standard burger van, so the little hot-dog trailer was perfect. And it established our stainless-steel theme. But it weighed a ton and a half, and it needed a V12 engine to tow it. We soon realised why it was being sold – it didn't even have a handbrake.'

Tony had no idea how to tow a trailer. And, for the first month of business, it took him half an hour to reverse the thing into the lock-up. It didn't help that he was using a British towbar and an American tow-hitch. 'It wasn't a very tight fit,' he says. 'One day I was driving along with my mate Kirky, and I took a right turn. Kirky said "It's come off". I said, "What's come off?". He said, "The trailer." When I went right, the trailer had just gone straight on. It was like something from *Some Mothers Do 'Ave 'Em.'*

The trailer wasn't safe when it was moving – but it wasn't much safer when it was stationary. Vandals took a fancy to its heavy metal side panels. As scrap, they were worth £5. But they cost Tony £300 to replace. The trailer had its hubcaps stolen, it was tagged by a graffiti artist (200 times), and – once – it was filled with fireworks. That was while it was parked next to Edinburgh University. 'I looked at everything that was happening,' says Tony, 'and I thought "Where is this business really going? Really. What are we going to do?"'

Tony had booked Stoats into all the music festivals. But offering a choice of nine different flavours made things difficult. 'If we only did three, we would have done so much better,' he says. 'It would be: "Slap, there you go." But that doesn't sit well with what we do. We get people saying, "Can I have some almonds on my cranachan, please? And an extra spoonful of cream?" It does take a wee bit longer, but that's what they're paying for. Which is £4.50 for a bowl of porridge. They could make it at home for a lot less. But they know that what they're buying from us is special.'

Bob and Tony were still having fun. 'Good times,' says Tony. 'We had a huge queue, made some money and partied a bit.' But there were unexpected stresses. 'There's just so much to remember when you're doing the festivals,' he says. 'It was all: "Did you bring the extra light for the van?" And: "Have you got that power cable?" We soon learnt that the last thing you need is your kit breaking. "Sorry, we can't make porridge – the burner's gone." So you take your own

spares. Ben from Tea And Toast, in Bristol, brings a spare water pump – and a spare spare in case his spare breaks.'

In the first year of operations, Tony and Bob took the Stoats trailer to eight festivals. 'I learnt to have a £200 contingency for the tyre that bursts. As it does. And then the engine goes, or the cylinder heads go. I used to get so wound up about it. But now I'm much calmer. We have vehicles guaranteed to get us there and back. We buy them new, and change them after four years – we don't need the hassle. It's all very well turning up in old-school campers, but they're just a pain in the arse and another thing to worry about.'

Stoats has become a family. It's not just Tony and Bob any more. Which means health insurance and pay roll – all the grown-up stuff. 'As soon as you bring staff in, it changes everything,' says Tony. 'Bob and I now need to lead by example. And I don't like sounding corporate, but we've got a brand to protect. We don't want someone in a Stoats uniform having a cigarette out the back, or rolling round drunk. We've gone from a £60,000- to a £600,000-turnover business in five years. And that's great. But our worries and woes have grown accordingly.'

It's not getting any easier to make money at the festivals. Especially with the rents going up and up. 'If you're selling meat in a roll,' says Tony, 'you can churn it out. And you're busy throughout the day. But there's a lower spend on a breakfast item – like porridge. So we have to negotiate hard over our rent at the festivals. If a crêpe van or a Mexican food truck refuses to pay a high rent, there's somebody else out there who will. But we're unique. We sell porridge. We negotiate over the fact that we bring something a bit different to the table.'

Tony now reckons that starting off in trailers was a bad idea. It required too much investment.

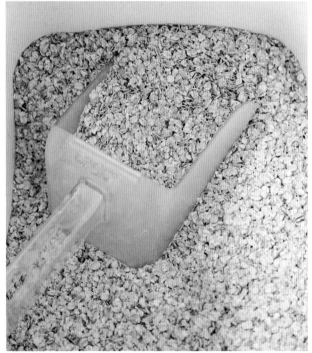

Each new van – lined with stainless steel to make it look like the original hot-dog trailer – cost £25,000. They were too expensive. They required a lot of start-up capital, which Stoats just didn't have. So the business grew, slowly, and Bob and Tony couldn't work out how to grow it any more quickly. 'We couldn't scale it – we couldn't grow it as quickly as we wanted to into a company with a £5million turnover.'

Tony won't stop trading at festivals and farmers' markets – he has decided that the idea of fresh porridge will always be a vital part of the Stoats brand identity. But he's always wanted to create a year-round business. Festivals, after all, have only a three- or four-month season in Scotland (no one wants to camp in November), and it's not worth keeping on staff to work a few farmers' markets over the winter. So Tony decided to rewrite the Stoats business plan. He chose to create a range of Stoats cereals, cookies and oatcakes.

Ironic really. In the beginning, Tony and Bob dreamt of having bars selling porridge dotted all over the UK – including Heathrow, Gatwick and St Pancras. Now they want to have Stoats porridge (and the Stoats porridge range) on sale in those places, but they don't want to be there selling them. 'All I know for sure is that I don't want to be driving for four hours to sell porridge at a music festival when I'm 50,' says Tony. 'I want to get someone else to do it for me. If I'm being brutally honest, I want to get rich and retire. Is that really so bad?'

# STOATS CRANACHAN PORRIDGE

This isn't something you'll see too often – a Scotsman admitting that he puts milk in his porridge. But Tony isn't your average Scot…

**Serves as many as you like**

Stoats porridge oat blend or rolled oats (50g per person)

Demerara sugar (20g per person)

Water (200ml per person)

Semi-skimmed milk (50ml per person)

Sea salt

Clear runny honey (2–3 teaspoons per person)

Fresh raspberries (40–50g per person)

Raspberry coulis (whole raspberries blitzed down)

Single cream

Preheat the oven to 180°C/gas mark 4.

Prepare the sweet toasted oats: scatter a thin layer of oats onto a baking tray and sprinkle with the demerara sugar. Place in middle of the oven for 15 minutes, folding the oats and sugar together regularly until they have turned golden brown. Cool.

For the porridge, add the water and milk to a non-stick saucepan with a small pinch of sea salt. Sprinkle in most of the toasted oats (save some for decoration) and heat on medium temperature. Bring to the boil, allowing the thickening porridge to bubble gently. Keep stirring, and simmer on a low heat for 5–10 minutes.

Once the liquid has been absorbed, remove from the heat and place a lid on top. Leave for a few minutes.

Remove the lid from the porridge and lightly mix in a squeeze of honey, fresh raspberries, raspberry coulis and single cream to give a marbled effect. Scoop the porridge into bowls.

To finish, sprinkle the reserved toasted oats over the porridge and top with a raspberry in the centre.

# OAT CRUNCH

This is delicious for breakfast in a bowl with cold or hot milk, or sprinkled over yogurt. A great way to use up store-cupboard fruit and nuts.

**Makes about 15 portions**

500g jumbo oats

400g desiccated coconut

400g slivered almonds

350g clear runny honey

100g sunflower seeds

50g pumpkin seeds

40g sesame seeds

70g mixed nuts (e.g. hazelnuts and Brazil nuts)

100g sultanas

50g dried cranberries

Preheat the oven to 150°C/gas mark 2.

Mix the jumbo oats, desiccated coconut and slivered almonds in a bowl. Heat the clear honey in a microwave and add to the dry mixture. Stir well to combine.

Place the mixture on non-stick baking trays and put in the oven for about 20 minutes or until it starts to turn golden.

Remove the trays from the oven and allow to cool. When the trays are cool enough to touch, slide the oat crunch into a bowl. Add the following to the bowl and mix well: the sunflower seeds, pumpkin seeds, sesame seeds, mixed nuts, sultanas and dried cranberries.

Store in an airtight container for up to 2 weeks.

# SMALL BITES

## Healthy Yummies
### Greengages

The culture of kitchen aggression is widespread. Raymond Blanc had his nose, cheek and jaw broken as a young chef when a colleague threw a saucepan at him. It's almost part of the training. It's why Marco Pierre White could cut one chef's apron off his back when he complained of the heat, and string another one up before dumping him in the bin for a 'time out', without getting hauled up in front of an employment tribunal. Chefs are a law unto themselves. And they're not interested in contractual smallprint.

Nichola Smith from Healthy Yummies isn't like that. She's mild-mannered and into co-operative working. The restaurant kitchen wasn't the place for her. 'And I had assumed that all chefs were passionate about food,' she says. 'But I was wrong. A lot of them started out as kitchen porters and worked their way up. So they didn't give two hoots about where the food came from — or what it had in it. To them, being a chef was just a job. And I came away broken-hearted. It was like finding out there's no Santa Claus. But it was the wake-up call I needed to get out.'

Before she worked in restaurant kitchens, Nichola had run her own place — a little bar in Majorca. And she ran it with passion and soul, picking up supplies from a local organic farm on the way to work. 'I used to cook something and send it out,' she says. 'There was a little curtain that divided the kitchen from the restaurant, and I would go and have a look at the reaction. I got such a buzz out of it, with the customers going: "Wow! How has she done that?" Nichola wanted to get that feeling back again. And she planned to do it with Healthy Yummies.

Nichola was well connected — and had a lot of friends in the media. 'To help me get the business off the ground, a few people asked me to cater their fashion shoots,' she says. 'I was looking up catering supplies online one day — foil and clingfilm, that sort of thing — when this old Bedford ice-cream van popped up. It had only 10,000 miles on the clock. It had a griddle, a fridge and a water heater. And it was exactly what I needed. The owner had someone coming to see the van at 11am the next day, so I got up at 5am, barged straight in and gazumped them.'

# HEALTHY YUMMIES

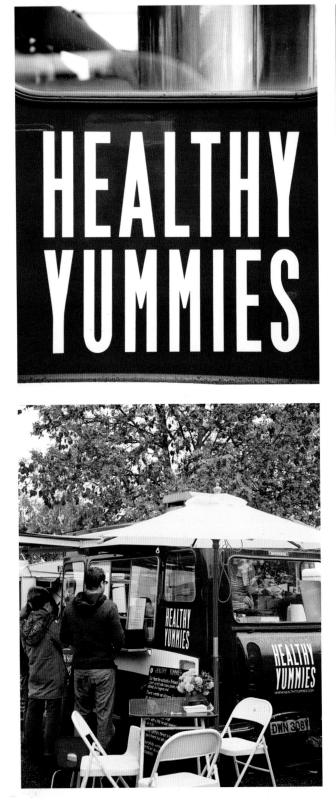

HEALTHY
YUMMIES

HEALTHY
YUMMIES
WWW.HEALTHYYUMMIES.COM

## MENU

DIVER CAUGHT
DORSET SCALLOPS,
CELERIAC PUREE,
OLD SPOT BACON
&
SEASHORE
VEGETABLES

# The van, christened Elvira May, has something magical about her.

The van – christened Elvira May after her Nan – has something magical about her. Even when she broke down (well, Nichola filled her up with diesel rather than petrol) Elvira May still managed to attract work. 'She was being loaded onto an AA van, and some guys from a production company – one Friday night in Shoreditch – said, 'My God, your van is amazing' and asked me to cater a Paloma Faith shoot the following week. I said "Are you serious? She's being lifted by the AA." But they were.' And Elvira hasn't stopped working since.

One of the highlights was winning Best Snack in the British Street Food Awards for hand-dived scallops and foraged sea vegetables – even though Nichola didn't know until the day before the finals whether the seas off Dorset would be calm enough for scallop diving. 'We ended up collecting the scallops from the fisherman at stupid o'clock on our way to the Awards,' she says. 'At a lay-by off the M40 – I always meet him in strange places. But he will only sell hand-dived,

and he's passionate about what he does. We need people like that in the world.'

Healthy Yummies has gone on to cater for various supermodels. And for video shoots for Plan B, Mark Ronson and Diana Vickers. Today, however, it's an ad campaign for McDonalds, and Elvira May has been left at home. Nichola and the Healthy Yummies team are working from a Routemaster – a double-decker London bus. The open platform, while exposed to the elements, allows boarding and alighting in 1950s style. And easy access to Nichola's shepherd's pie.

It's 30 minutes until the lunch break, but the kitchens remain calm. A lot of caterers serve up 'cruise food' – dishes that don't mind standing around. They know that oven-cooked pasta dishes – such as lasagne or cannelloni – work really well, and sit in a bain-marie to keep warm. But Nichola doesn't operate like that. She likes to serve food 'à la minute' – it's her restaurant training. It's only when Toby, her head chef, gets a call that the advert will be breaking ten minutes early that Nichola fires up the ovens. For a moment, the calm is lost.

The shepherd's pie is made with lamb from Blackwells Farm in the Essex Colne Valley. 'I cooked it off an hour ago,' says Nichola, 'with no seasoning, no nothing, and it tasted incredible. So we've done very little to it. And we're serving it with a selection of lovely, fresh vegetables and salads.' It's not a heavy lunch. Which is another point of difference between Healthy Yummies and other catering companies – they don't overload the carbohydrates. 'People have got to go back to work,' says Nichola. 'And not fall asleep. So we work hard to get the balance right.'

The peas are fresh, and green. The heritage carrots taste of the soil – not a polytunnel. They're a reminder of the olden days, when soft, sweet strawberries yielded their stalks with the lightest of tugs because they were expected to

# The Healthy Yummies way is all about the personal little touches.

last only a day before they were turned into jam. The olden days when tomatoes were bred for taste. Nowadays they're bred for convenience. They have to last months in cold storage – and are shipped across continents before they are 'forced to ripeness' with a mix of gases. That's not the Healthy Yummies way.

The Healthy Yummies way is all about the personal little touches. The tables are set with linen and fresh flowers. And it's the nice tea, not the cheap stuff. Nichola catered a Biffy Clyro video shoot – late at night, in a dark forest. She cooked pork, early in the evening, but kept hold of the skin. In the early hours of the morning, she cooked it, and took the crackling onto the set for a little pick-me-up. 'Good-old-fashioned treats never fail,' she says. 'And the forest was covered in wild garlic, so we grabbed as much as we could for lunch the next day.'

Nichola won't compromise on quality. 'I can't,' she says. 'I would rather stop trading. Quality is what Healthy Yummies is all about. I've just got to find a way to make it all financially viable. It's difficult. We've got to be out every day – at the moment we're out three times a week. And any money we make goes on a new bit of kit. Like heavy-duty Easy Ups. They're pop-up tents – we go through four of them a month. And we need a new fridge freezer. The list of stuff we need is never ending. My Mum had to resort to buying me a van heater for Christmas.'

The Routemaster is an additional challenge. Nichola has just discovered there are no thermostats on the oven. The pipes were frost damaged, because they weren't properly lagged, so the seals went and water leaked everywhere. 'When you're a caterer,' says Nichola, 'it doesn't matter what the problem is – it's your fault. People don't care about your issues with electricity. And they don't care if there's flooding.

The food has got to be out there on time. I still get a kick out of it, but it can be a nightmare.'

The owner of the Routemaster has offered to sell it to Nichola. But she's not interested. Like Elvira May, it's charming. 'We love the Routemaster, but it's not really what we need,' she says. 'When you're getting up at 3am, you don't need that little voice in the back of your head going: "Is it going to start?" You've spent most of the budget on supplies, and if you can't get there you've got to swallow that cost yourself.'

A trailer is an option – but they're not great when you need to get into tight spots. Like today. The McDonalds car park on London's busy Wandsworth Bridge Road isn't the place to be engaging in complicated manoeuvres. She's tried towing trailers before and it didn't go well. 'Getting up at long before dawn, you just want to jump into something warm and go. Not get out and hook the whole thing up.' So Nichola is looking at buying a brand-new truck. And doing something creative with the paint job. 'But Elvira will always sum up what Healthy Yummies is about.'

Matt Timms at Greengages settled on a classic Morgan Olson. This aluminum-bodied truck originated in Brooklyn more than 60 years ago, when the owner of a laundry complained to a friend that their steel truck bodies were just too heavy. It's now an American design icon, and one of the most popular shells for US food trucks. But it's still a rarity over here. Which is why Matt liked the idea. 'I had it fitted out in the USA,' he says, 'but I wanted the paint job to be done in Britain.' That was probably a mistake.

Matt was in a meeting the day the colour test was done on the van. 'Having checked the colour samples I thought it would be a subtler green,' he says. But it wasn't. 'When I went back to the spray shop I wasn't expecting it to be so vibrant. But it's calmed down a lot since then. And now it works

well for us. It stands out from the crowd. It's a real head-turner.' Matt had gone from working in professional restaurant kitchens to field kitchens for catering companies. And he was tired of dragging ovens round. And setting up kitchens in the middle of nowhere. 'I wanted a restaurant-style kitchen that I could move round where I wanted,' says Matt. 'And cook what I wanted. Now I'm happy.'

It wasn't glamorous to begin with. Far from it. Greengages started off trading in a lay-by. A pretty lay-by – on a windy road in the Peak District, between Bakewell and Matlock – but a lay-by nonetheless. 'There has always been someone trading on it,' says Matt. 'We found out that, just after the war, two desert rats parked there, serving basic food. So we had regulars – quite a few walkers and climbers.' But Matt didn't want to get labelled as just another roadside café. So, after nine months, he shut the hatch. And drove on.

Now he's doing street food markets and event catering. All with the 'help' of his young family. But the real key to Greengages' success is Matt's high-end food theatre. He makes pasta in front of his customers, for instance. And bakes bread. 'It draws people in,' he says. 'They can see the dough proving on top of the oven. They can see the chef rolling it out. And they can see the bread coming out of the oven. A slice or two, with some good dry-cured bacon and a free-range egg – people will queue for hours for that.'

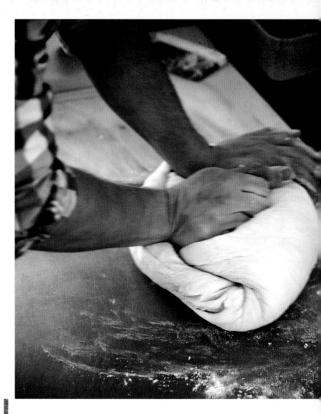

# PUMPKIN SOUP

To keep this Greengages soup local, Matt – from Derbyshire – goes for either Skylark goat's cheese from Nottingham or Innes goat's cheese from Staffordshire.

**Serves 4**

1kg pumpkin

50g butter

2 tablespoons olive oil

2 white English onions, roughly chopped

2 garlic cloves, roughly chopped

1 thumb-sized piece of fresh ginger, peeled and roughly chopped

2 celery sticks, plus any celery leaves, roughly chopped

1 rosemary sprig

2 litres vegetable stock

1 teaspoon cumin seeds

Sea salt and freshly ground black pepper

Pinch of grated nutmeg

Remove all the seeds from the pumpkin with a tablespoon. Remove all the fibrous flesh from the seeds and set aside. Peel and chop the pumpkin.

Heat the butter and 1 tablespoon of the olive oil in a large saucepan. Add the onions, garlic, ginger, celery and rosemary and cook for 2 minutes. Reduce the heat and cook, without browning, for 10 minutes. Add the pumpkin and cook for a further 5 minutes. Add the vegetable stock and cook on a low to medium heat for 25–30 minutes until the pumpkin is cooked through.

Meanwhile, heat a dry pan, add the pumpkin seeds and roast for 5 minutes. Add the remaining tablespoon of olive oil to the pan and very slowly cook the seeds until crisp and dark brown. At the very last minute throw in the cumin seeds, cook for 1 minute and remove to a piece of kitchen paper to drain.

Transfer all the solids to a blender and add just enough of the liquid to allow the soup to blend to a nice thick purée. Season with some sea salt, freshly ground pepper and nutmeg. If you want to let the soup down a little more, just add a bit more cooking liquid. Reserve the leftover liquid as stock for later use.

Sprinkle the crisp pumpkin seeds over the finished soup and serve.

# SCALLOPS, CELERIAC PURÉE, BACON & SEASHORE VEGETABLES

This dish – voted Best Snack in the British Street Food Awards – won over all the judges. Nichola of Healthy Yummies likes to think that 'it's like being wrapped up in a cashmere blanket and having a little pinch on the bum by Johnny Depp to boot!'

Scallops are generally at their best between July and September. This is (weather permitting) the time before they spawn, thereby producing wonderfully plump corals. As a diver, Nichola has first-hand experience of the destruction of the seabed that dredging for scallops causes. Good fishmongers will stock the diver-caught scallops.

### Serves 8

1 medium celeriac

600ml whole milk

200ml double cream

1 bay leaf

1 thyme sprig

¼ teaspoon freshly grated nutmeg

Salt and freshly ground black pepper

150g seashore vegetables (Nichola uses sea beet, sea purslane, stone-crop and samphire. If you can't get hold of all of them, samphire alone is great)

8 large diver-caught scallops, plus shells (cleaned)

2 rashers of Gloucester Old Spot smoked streaky bacon, finely diced

1 tablespoon mild olive oil

40g good-quality butter, cut into cubes

1 lemon, halved

Peel the celeriac and cut into 2cm cubes. Put the celeriac, milk, cream, bay leaf, thyme and nutmeg into a pan and cook on a medium heat with the lid on, until the celeriac is soft. Remove from the heat, take out the herbs and blend the celeriac with a little of the liquor in batches until all the celeriac is used up. You should have a purée consistency – adjust with the liquor accordingly. Add salt and pepper to taste and set aside.

Sort through the seashore vegetables and pick out any woody stalks, then set aside.

Wash the scallops and place them in between two pieces of kitchen paper to absorb any excess water.

Add the bacon to a hot frying pan without oil and toss for 2–3 minutes until just cooked. Remove, place on kitchen paper and set aside.

When you are ready to cook the dish, it will take 2 minutes, so have your components by the stove. Put the celeriac purée in a pan and gently heat through. Season both sides of the scallops well. Have the scallop shells ready.

Put a large frying pan on a medium heat until just before smoking and then add the oil and scallops. Do not move them around – let them caramelise.

While the scallops are on, place 1 dessertspoon of the celeriac purée into each shell. After 1 minute, or when the underside of the scallops has browned, turn the scallops over and add the bacon. After 30 seconds, add the butter and squeeze in the lemon juice (this will brown a little, which is good). When the butter has melted, add the seashore vegetables and toss a little. Turn the heat off. Place one scallop on top of the celeriac purée in each shell, followed by a spoon of the brown butter with bacon and finally the seashore vegetables.

# SEARED BAVETTE STEAK WITH SUMMER SALAD

Bavette steak is a rarely used cut of meat, but full of flavour if it's cooked well. It's a relatively long, flat cut from the abdominal muscles of the cow. By just searing this cut you retain all the flavours and juice. Healthy Yummies like to serve it on a bed of summer vegetables.

**Serves 4**

2 green courgettes

2 yellow courgettes

200ml mild olive oil

Salt and freshly ground black pepper

8 asparagus spears

grated zest and juice of 1 large unwaxed lemon

800g bavette steak

250g frozen petits pois, defrosted

50g rocket

150g feta cheese

50g pea shoots

Place a griddle on the stove at a high heat.

Using a potato peeler or mandolin, peel strips off each courgette lengthways, about 2–3mm thick. Place in a bowl and pour in around 50ml of the oil. Add some seasoning and mix, making sure each strip is coated.

Break off the ends of the asparagus spears (they will naturally break where the fibrous bit stops) and set aside. If the spears are large, cut in half lengthways.

When the griddle is smoking, add the strips of courgette in one layer. As soon as they are bar marked, turn them over. When they are done, take them off and place in a large mixing bowl. Continue grilling the courgette strips until they are all done. Mix the asparagus in the remaining seasoned oil from the courgettes and place on the griddle, turning until bar marked all around. Add these to the courgettes.

Place the remaining oil (less a glug for the meat) in a bowl and mix in the lemon zest and juice along with plenty of salt and pepper.

Preheat the oven to 180°C/gas mark 4.

Trim off all the surplus fat and sinew from the bavette and season heavily with salt and pepper. Put a large frying pan on a medium heat (one that you can later put in the oven; if you don't have one, use an oven tray). When the pan is smoking, add a glug of oil and the bavette steak. Sear the meat until brown on both sides, and place in the oven for 5–6 minutes. (The thickness of the meat can vary. If it's particularly thin, you may not need to put it in the oven.)

Meanwhile, mix the peas in with the courgettes and asparagus, add the rocket and crumble in the feta. Remove the meat from the oven and let it rest for 5 minutes. It is very important to rest the meat for around the same amount of time it takes to cook it.

Transfer the steak to a chopping board and, with a very sharp and thin knife, cut against the grain into very thin slices.

Coat the salad with the lemon dressing and place on a serving platter with the steak on top. Garnish with the pea shoots.

# MACKEREL, BEETROOT & HORSERADISH ON RYE

Mackerel is a highly sustainable fish. The marriage of flavours in this Healthy Yummies recipe is spot on, and the diversity of colour makes it very pleasing to the eye. This dish can be eaten as a canapé, starter or light main.

**Makes around 10 canapés**

>   1 large uncooked beetroot, about 150g
>
>   1 tablespoon mild olive oil
>
>   Maldon sea salt and freshly ground black pepper
>
>   150g smoked mackerel (if you can find a fishmonger to supply a whole naturally smoked mackerel, it will taste infinitely better)
>
>   1 teaspoon lemon juice (optional)
>
>   Rye bread
>
>   A few chives
>
>   100ml double cream
>
>   1–2 teaspoons freshly grated horseradish
>
>   Mustard cress, to garnish

Preheat the oven to 180°C/gas mark 4.

Wash and dry the beetroot and brush with the oil. Place on a piece of foil on top of a large pinch of salt. Seal the foil so that it's airtight and place in the oven for around 45 minutes or until a knife can penetrate the beetroot easily. It's good to have a bite to the beetroot and not overdo it. Set aside to cool.

Turn the oven down to 160°C/gas mark 3.

Remove the skin and bones of the mackerel and place it in a bowl. The flesh will break up as you are removing the bones, which is fine. Season with pepper, and if you are not using a whole smoked fish, add a little lemon juice to taste at this point too. Mix and set aside.

Remove the crust from the rye bread and cut into 5mm slices. Cut each slice into rectangles around 2.5 x 5cm. Place these on a baking tray and put into the oven for around 15 minutes, turning once. The time will vary depending on the moisture content of the bread. Do check continually until you have nice crisp croûtons. Set aside to cool.

Using a pair of gloves, remove the skin of the beetroot and cut into 5mm slices. Cut each slice into 5mm cubes. Very finely chop a few strands of chive and mix through.

Using a handheld electric mixer, whisk the double cream in a bowl until it is thick, then mix in the horseradish and some pepper. Put the mixture into a piping bag and refrigerate.

To assemble, put a teaspoon of the fish onto one end of each rye toast and fill the other end with the diced beetroot. Pipe a spot of the horseradish mousse on top, adding a few strands of mustard cress to garnish.

# TOMATO, LOVAGE & BRAISED CELERY CROSTINI

Healthy Yummies puts this on the menu only in the summer when all the ingredients are at their very best. Lovage, tomatoes and celery are a match made in heaven and beautifully British. Nichola says, 'Any tomato can be used, but, when in season, heritage tomatoes are packed with flavour, and the diversity in colour makes these canapés look even more beautiful.'

**Makes around 10 canapés**

   ½ celery stick

   Ground Maldon salt and freshly ground
   black pepper

   250g heritage tomatoes

   2 tablespoons rapeseed oil,
   plus extra for drizzling

   ½ teaspoon Sarsons malt vinegar

   ¼ ficelle (thin baguette)

   10 lovage leaves, finely chopped

Preheat the oven to 200°C/gas mark 6.

Using a peeler, peel away the stringy part of the celery. Place in a small pan, cover with water and add 1 teaspoon of freshly ground black pepper. Bring to the boil and simmer for 20 minutes or until the celery is

*al dente*. Drain and cool. Cut into 3cm pieces and then into fine strips as thick as matchsticks. Set aside.

Fill a bowl with icy water. Using a knife, make a cross at the top of each tomato. Bring a pan of water to the boil and add the tomatoes for 12 seconds. (If they are of different sizes, bear in mind that the smaller ones will need less time.) Plunge the tomatoes into the cold water. Peel off the skins, quarter and take out the seeds so that you are left with the outer tomato flesh only. Put a J-cloth on a tray, spread the tomato quarters on top and cover with another J-cloth and a tray. Press down gently and leave for 20 minutes. This removes surplus water from the tomatoes to prevent them bleeding; it also enables them to take on the dressing.

Mix 2 tablespoons rapeseed oil with the vinegar and set aside. Slice the bread on a 90-degree angle; each slice around 3–4mm thick. Arrange on a baking tray and drizzle rapeseed oil over each piece. Season with salt and bake in the oven for around 5–10 minutes, or until golden. Remove from the oven and cool. These croûtons can be made well in advance if you wish, and stored in an airtight container.

Place the tomato quarters on a chopping board and cut into 5mm strips. Turn the strips and cut again to give 5mm dice. Add the tomatoes to the vinegar dressing. Mix in a pinch of Maldon salt and the lovage.

To assemble, spoon the diced tomatoes (around 10g) onto each croûton and place two celery strips on top.

# FESTIVE NOUGAT

This recipe relies on chemistry but the result is incredibly satisfying. Nichola of Healthy Yummies promises the recipe has been laboriously tried and tested, and is 'guaranteed to put a smile on your face'. Don't attempt it without a sugar thermometer or it won't work.

**Makes 5 strips or 20 squares**

Vegetable oil, for greasing

2 large sheets of rice paper

100g pistachio nuts

100g hazelnuts

175g clear runny honey

300g unrefined caster sugar

50g liquid glucose (optional, but stops the sugar from crystallising on cooling)

1 tablespoon orange blossom water

2 tablespoons water

2 large egg whites

Pinch of salt

100g dried cranberries

Preheat the oven to 180°C/gas mark 4. Grease a 15cm square tin with a little vegetable oil and line the base and sides with rice paper.

Very lightly toast the pistachios and hazelnuts in the oven for 5–10 minutes until just darkening, turning often. Remove from the oven and cool. Chop roughly.

Place the honey, sugar, glucose, orange blossom water and water in a pan and heat slowly until the sugar has dissolved. Stir occasionally. Turn up the heat, bring to the boil, then cook the mixture until it reaches 157°C on a sugar thermometer. This will take around 10 minutes. Remove from the heat.

Whisk the egg whites with a pinch of salt in a large heatproof bowl until they form soft peaks. Slowly add the hot mixture while still whisking. Keep whisking until the mixture thickens and darkens. Add the cranberries and nuts, stir and spoon into the tin. Press a sheet of rice paper over the top and set aside to cool.

Once the mixture has cooled, refrigerate overnight.

Tip the nougat onto a board and cut to your required size.

# BURGERS

## The Meatwagon

Standing in The Meatwagon burger van, Yianni Papoutsis has an air of menace about him. He's wearing grey camouflage trousers and a black t-shirt, with a skull-and-crossbones bandana. 'I've had chefs pass out behind this griddle,' he says. 'It gets up to 120 degrees – it's like hell sometimes.' But that won't stop Yianni. In fact, he's just got back from Burning Man – an apocalyptic celebration of self-expression in the American desert. 'Like they say, if you can't stand the heat, get out of the kitchen.'

When he first set up The Meatwagon – which serves the best burgers in Britain – Yianni used to wear chef's whites. Then he went to Burning Man, and 'found himself' in the desert. 'All of a sudden it felt like I was doing it under false pretences. I needed to bring it back to what it actually was – a burger van. That was staffed by a bunch of ordinary blokes who liked having a good time, a drink, and a bit of banter. After Burning Man, the whites didn't seem right any more.'

Yianni took the whole thing back to basics. 'The Meatwagon is a burger van that sells burgers,' he says. 'There will, maybe, at some point be a logo on the side. If we really need one. But at the moment we don't. The first van was just a white box with a griddle in it. The second van is a silver box with a few more griddles in it. That's all there is. It's not trying to pretend to be a three-star dining experience. We make burgers – we just happen to make them very well indeed.'

It's a full-on life – and The Meatwagon's round of private parties and festivals is hard work. The team don't just turn up and start cooking. 'Before a job,' says Yianni, 'you've got to prep the van and, if you're driving anywhere, you've got to stow everything like you're on a ship. You strap everything down. Then you've got to fill up your water and stock up on your propane. There's lots of physical work – and most chefs just won't do it. The job isn't right for everyone.'

Yianni is used to hard graft. When he was working with touring ballet companies – everyone from the English National Ballet to the Michael Clark Company – he was always the 'go-to guy'. He was in charge of erecting the stage and putting up the lighting. 'All the mechanical stuff,' he says. 'I would fly dancers through the air,

# A juicy, two-fisted burger provides comfort. It isn't a trend – it's a classic.

if necessary. And then I would load the trucks at the end of the night. I just liked getting my hands dirty.'

While on tour in Denmark, he found out that – if he played with the tv aerial on the tour bus – he could get a decent picture for *Ready, Steady, Cook*. By watching the Red Tomatoes versus the Green Peppers, he learnt how to use a knife. 'And reduce a stock,' says Yianni. He started to cook more regularly, and more confidently, and his circle of friends seemed to approve. They especially liked his burgers. 'In fact,' he says, 'they all reckoned that I should go and open a restaurant of my own.'

He could see that the world of ballet was changing. 'I liked dragging bits of steel around,' he says. 'But, slowly, everything was being computerised.' Yianni decided that he would get out. His back was playing up, and he wanted to be at home with his family for more than two months of the year. 'Plus, if I'm honest, I never really liked ballet in the first place. So I made a plan – I had two years to find something I really enjoyed.'

Yianni had always travelled. Even after he'd just got back from travelling. 'When you're on tour for six months at at time, with 150 people, it drives you nuts. You've got no private life. No personal space. So I would finish a tour and go away on my own. Towards the end of my time in the ballet I went to the Maine lobster festival. It was on US Highway One – the strip of road that runs from Canada down to Key West. Flashing neon lights, 24-hour service stations, strip clubs and diners. I loved it.'

A lobster tail with mayonnaise, in a hot-dog bun, was the beginning of Yianni's love affair with US street food. 'It was one of the most sublime dining experiences I've ever had,' he says. 'The sweet tails were selling for a few bucks. At Ed's Lobster Bar in New York you're looking at six times that, for something that's not as good. This guy was operating out of an old caravan. From the minute he opened to the minute he closed, he had a queue. Without Ed's seriously high rents. It started me thinking.'

He was still thinking by the time he reached Florida – and the little place where they served fresh clams. 'From a shed,' says Yianni. 'They were boiling clams in this huge metal drum. They put a paper cloth onto the table, and served up a bucket of clams and a cold beer. I went with the guy who owned the motel where I was staying, but I met an investment banker, the local mechanic, everyone. That's a big thing for me – the egalitarian nature of street food in America.'

The epicentre of the American street food scene has always been Los Angeles – a city that lives on the streets. One street food seller, outside the Staples Center, cooks bacon-wrapped hot dogs on shopping baskets topped with jerry-rigged griddles he has made from aluminium sheet pans. The whole rig can't cost him more than $20 to build – cheap enough to leave if the cops chase him off for selling food without a licence. But he keeps coming back.

When Yianni got to LA, he found a new type of mobiler – the big-time operater, with a plasma-screen menu. 'The flashier the truck, the worse the food,' he says. 'I ate at 24 trucks in four days. And the best food was served at some Mexican place with no name on it – a Mom-and-Pop operation, with a little menu on a sheet of cardboard. Two blocks down were the glitz mobiles with pumping sound systems and everything you would possibly want. Just nothing you would want to eat.'

He returned to the UK with an idea. And, as it happens, an ISA that wasn't earning any interest. 'I thought, "I don't have the necessary experience to open a restaurant, so I'll buy a trailer instead." ' And a cast iron griddle. 'I had to go to America to find one that was heavy enough to get that lovely caramelised crust on the meat. It was 40 years old.' But it was worth it. Three weeks after The Meatwagon opened, people were making the pilgrimage from all over Britain.

The Meatwagon doesn't have a menu – Yianni likes it that way. 'The advantage is that every single person has to come up and talk to us. We like that. First time you're a newbie, the second time you're a regular. We already know your name. That personal element.' He might offer something he's picked up at the butcher that morning (buffalo wings, for instance), but Yianni's burgers (cheese burger, bacon cheese burger and chili cheese burger) are the cornerstone of everything he does.

Yianni knows that, in troubled times, a juicy, two-fisted burger provides comfort. It isn't a trend – it's a classic. And it's a classic for a reason. So he doesn't monkey about with it. Yianni knows that the meat shouldn't be lean – otherwise you'll end up with a burger that's mealy and dry. And he knows that you've got to get your meat-to-bun ratio right. For those new to the burger game, it's usually a 1:1. But he's put a lot of extra research into creating the perfect burger.

There are no offcuts in a Meatwagon burger. Just whole joints of chuck steak, minced into a patty. 'I like a thick grind' says Yianni, 'so that when you bite into the burger you're biting into big chunks of meat. It's a textural thing.' The patty (a mix of 15 per cent fat and 85 per cent meat) is a little less fatty than a standard burger. If it were the standard 20 per cent fat, there would be lumps of hard fat inside which (because it's cooked quickly, and served pink) wouldn't have reached a high enough temperature to melt.

Don't ask Yianni to serve a burger well done. He won't like it. 'I'll explain that the burgers on The Meatwagon aren't made from the mince you buy in the supermarket – the mince that's hosed off the carcass, pounded into a slurry, and then oozed out into a vacuum pack. The meat I use was cut off the bone that morning. And I have enough trust in my meat to eat it raw. I'll eat it in front of customers – like steak tartare. Nine times out of ten people say, "All right then – I'll have it pink." '

To make the burger, Yianni takes a fistful of meat and presses it down onto the griddle to get the desired thickness. He adds salt and pepper, and turns it – once. Simple. 'But I didn't realise quite how complicated it is,' he says, 'until I had to teach it to someone else. I have cooked thousands of burgers. Everything from the way I spread the ketchup (he treats it not as a condiment but as a vital ingredient) to the way I get a pickle in every bite. It's in my muscle memory. But it's hard to teach.'

Ask Yianni about his suppliers and – all of a sudden – he goes quiet. Take his butcher. All Yianni will say is that he's well respected in the trade. And that he operates, in South London, from an anonymous building with no signage. 'All the best restaurants – one or two Michelin stars – use him. They get meat delivered in anonymous white vans, by guys with no markings

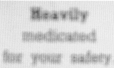

on their uniforms. They don't want other people to know who their suppliers are. You've got to protect your sources.'

He's not much more forthcoming about his bakery. Yianni had a taste for processed American burger buns. And he couldn't get them here. So he decided to work with a bakery, which has been in the business since the 17th century, to make his own. Real bread, which replicates the structure and flavour of a processed bun. It was a long experiment, during which the bread was too soft, too pale, too floury, too brown or too crusty. But they got there in the end. The whole process took a year.

'And I've had far too much fucking indigestion to tell anybody about my cheese,' says Yianni. He started off with a good mature Cheddar. 'We would steam it,' he says, 'and it would melt down onto the griddle. But it overwhelmed the meat.' So he kept looking. 'Every time I went to a shop I would buy a packet. We literally had an entire fridge that was nothing but cheese. I must have eaten 1,000 cheeses. So I won't tell you what cheese I use – you haven't suffered like I've suffered.'

Food purists still frown on the fact that Yianni's cheese is processed. But they are the purists who haven't eaten a Meatwagon burger. 'Cheddar, if you heat it, it will separate – oil on top, melted cheese solids underneath. American cheese is so homogenised that it can take extremes of temperature without splitting. I don't see the need to apologise for an ingredient that works perfectly. I wouldn't have it in a cheese sandwich, but on burgers it's perfect. And perfection is what I'm all about.'

On the seventh day, God rests. I barbecue. I take it so seriously, I was a judge at the World Championships in Memphis. It was the sort of place where the secrets of your sauce are protected by state law. But over here it often goes so badly wrong. Blackened hunks of meat, carbonised on the outside, raw and cold in the middle. The meat is often of a chemical-industrial provenance. And tastes of lighter fluid.

Yianni shares my pain: 'Shrivelled, carbonised discs, still frozen in the middle, drowned in ketchup and served on a cold, oversized bun by some gurning berk in a novelty apron clutching a plastic glass of Pimm's or some other revolting concoction that people seem to think it's prefectly acceptable to drink as soon as the sun comes out.' Luckily he's come up with the answer. Like most of Yianni's answers, it starts with freshly minced chuck steak. You'll also need real charcoal – 'None of this briquette crap,' he says.

His use of a thick, circular slice of onion is a classic touch in burger joints all over the States. In most cases the onion would be left raw, but here Yianni cooks it on the barbecue, to sweeten it up and mellow out the flavour. 'Always, always use processed American-style cheese slices,' he says. 'Don't use them for anything else, but on a burger no other cheese comes close. For the bun, get down to your local baker and ask him to bake you some soft white rolls, preferably with no flour on top: a dense, chewy texture means it'll probably stand up structurally to all the meat juices. And your butcher will be happy to grind you some chuck steak. If he's got anything dry-aged, so much the better.'

## Serves 1 drunken guest

A fistful of freshly minced chuck steak

Generous amounts of salt and pepper

1 cm-thick slice of a large white onion

1 burger bun

2 American-style processed cheese slices

Heinz tomato ketchup

French's mustard

A few slices of dill pickle (not the sweet ones)

Lots of cold beer

# BBQ'D BURGER

Light your charcoal. It's hot work, so grab yourself a beer to cool down.

The coals will need to burn down to cooking temperature and this will take a while. Use this opportunity to enjoy a couple more icy beers. You deserve them.

When the coals are coated with a white ash (they will glow red in the dark) and all the flames have died down, you're ready to cook. And quite likely drunk.

Pull out a wad of minced chuck steak and form it into a ball in your hands. It should fill both hands when cupped together. Squash this down onto a sheet of greaseproof paper so that it forms a burger-sized disc. It does not need to be a perfect circle.

Put it on the barbecue grill and season the top side with a healthy dose of salt and pepper.

Wash your hands after handling the meat: you don't want to get your beer bottle dirty.

Put the thick slice of onion on the barbecue, too.

Meanwhile, cut the bun in half and toast the cut sides over the barbecue. This will only take a few seconds.

When the bottom of the burger has formed a good brown crust, it will easily lift off the barbecue without sticking. Flip it and cook the other side. It won't take nearly as long. Flip the onion while you're at it.

Lay a couple of slices of 'cheese' over the burger while it's on the barbecue.

Layer the bottom of your bun with a squirt each of Heinz ketchup and French's mustard. Stick a couple of slices of dill pickle on there too.

Lay the burger onto your bun base and slap the cooked onion on top. The melted cheese will hold it in place.

Put the bun lid on top and serve immediately with the rest of the beer.

Note: This is an American recipe, and 'chili' is the American spelling. So please don't write letters. Chili has always had a special place in Yianni's heart – it was the first savoury dish he cooked from start to finish as a child. So when he went to the States, and ate his way round the dozens of regional variations, he was a happy man. 'The great thing about cooking chili is that you can really play around with the ingredients and have some fun: try adding chopped chipotles for a smoky flavour or use chopped fresh chilli peppers. You can add tomato purée and replace some of the beef stock with chopped tomatoes if you prefer the sweeter flavour of that particular kind of chili. I call this Layover Chili as it's made specifically to be served over other things. In Seattle they serve it over burgers, spaghetti, steak, fries – you name it, they'll put this chili on it. The idea is to end up with a smooth sauce rather than a lumpy stew, hence the slightly unusual cooking technique of boiling the ingredients in the stock without browning them first.'

# LAYOVER CHILI

### Serves 4–8 depending on what you have with it

- 1.8 litres beef stock
- 2 white onions, finely diced
- 3–4 large garlic cloves, minced
- 900g minced chuck steak
- 1 bottle ice-cold beer
- A handful of minced jalapeños
- A significant amount of ground cumin
- A large pinch each of chilli powder, cayenne pepper, paprika and black pepper
- A hefty sprinkle of ground coriander
- A good shake of dried oregano
- A squirt of tomato ketchup
- A similarly sized squirt of French's mustard
- Salt and pepper
- Grated cheese, minced onions and minced jalapeños to garnish (optional)

Add the beef stock to a large pan and get it boiling. Dump the onions and garlic in, followed by the beef, taking care not to scald yourself with boiling hot stock. The liquid should completely cover the meat. If it doesn't, add more.

Using a wooden spoon, break up the meat. This takes a while. Your arms will hurt. When the meat's broken up, open the beer. Drink the beer. Your arms will stop hurting. Add the minced jalapeños and all the dry spices. Don't add any salt – there's already loads in the stock.

Adjust the spicing to your taste, adding little bits at a time and letting it cook for 5 minutes before tasting. Don't be shy with the spicing: it's a chili, not a bolognese. You should be able to taste the earthy flavour of the cumin through the hot stuff. Adjust the balance with a couple of squirts of ketchup and mustard.

Keep the chili simmering over a low heat for at least a couple of hours: the longer, the better. Stir it occasionally.

Now's the time to adjust the seasoning with a bit of salt and pepper. Once again – go easy on the salt.

Ideally, let it rest for at least an hour after cooking. This actually gets significantly better if you leave it overnight and eat it the following day.

Serve over nachos, hot dogs, spaghetti, burgers – whatever, really. Top with grated cheese, minced jalapeños and some minced white onions if you like.

# MEATLOAF

Meatloaf is a real American classic. But the British have never quite got the hang of it. 'My only experience of it,' says Yianni, 'was what they served us at school – a grey, tasteless slice of unidentifiable animal(?) protein with the consistency of… words actually fail me.' But at a small family-owned diner outside an amusement park in New England, his life changed. 'Taking a seat at the counter, I ordered a root beer (served ice cold in plastic beakers) and asked the waitress what she'd recommend. 'Meatloaf,' she replied instantly. I took her advice and was presented with a huge slab of meatloaf, propped up against a mountain of mashed potato and drowned in gravy. Real gravy with bits in it. There may have been vegetables. I'm not the person to ask. It was great. A real eye-opener. Moist, full of beefy flavour and smothered in a delicious sweet-and-sour glaze. This was one of those rare moments when a dish tastes exactly how you'd imagined and wished it would. If you've got a load of mince and feel like something more 'solid' than a bolognese or a chili, this is a really hearty (and cheap) way of feeding four to six hungry mouths.'

## Serves 4–6

3 garlic cloves, finely chopped

1 onion, finely chopped

1 carrot, finely chopped

1 celery stick, finely chopped

1 red pepper, deseeded and finely grated

Splash of olive oil

A small knob of butter

1 kg minced chuck steak

50g breadcrumbs

2 eggs, beaten

A good dose of Worcestershire sauce

A couple of pinches of salt

Generous sprinkling of freshly ground black pepper

Pinch of cayenne pepper

Pinch of chilli powder

A couple of pinches of dried mixed herbs (Italian mix works well)

### For the glaze

2 tablespoons brown sugar

2 tablespoons tomato ketchup

2 tablespoons Dijon mustard

Preheat the oven to 180°C/gas mark 4.

Sweat the garlic, onion, carrot, celery and red pepper in a frying pan over a low heat in the olive oil and butter for 5–6 minutes until the onion is translucent, being careful not to burn the garlic. (You can always add the garlic half way through if you don't trust yourself.)

When it is cool enough to handle, add the vegetable mixture to the minced chuck steak together with the rest of the meatloaf ingredients. Mix well with your hands.

At this point you can either put the mixture into a greased 1.5-litre loaf tin or form it into a loaf shape on a greased baking tray, depending on what you've got to hand and how you want it to look. Wet your hands slightly to stop the mix sticking to them.

Put the loaf in the oven for about 30 minutes. Meanwhile, get the glaze ready – simply mix the sugar, ketchup and mustard together in a bowl.

Remove the loaf and spread the glaze over the top. Get it back into the oven for another 30 minutes or so. If you've got a meat thermometer, the centre should reach 70°C.

Remove the loaf when it's done and let it cool for half an hour. If you try to cut it before it's had a chance to rest it'll just fall to bits.

Cut into slices and serve with mashed potatoes and steamed vegetables.

Alternatively it's great, hot or cold, in sandwiches, ideally toasted with some Swiss cheese, mustard and gherkins (which is how we serve it at The Meatwagon.)

# THE GARBAGE PLATE

The original American garbage plate is made with home fries and macaroni salad topped with a couple of burgers smothered in cheese and sauces and hails from Rochester, New York. Yianni's version is a little different. Inspired by a dish served at his local fast food café when he was living in Denmark, this also takes some influences from steak tartare. 'The pickles cut through the grease,' he says, 'and halfway through you'll be left with a gooey-but-oh-so-tasty mess. It tastes best at about 3am with a belly full of beer.'

## Serves 1

A portion of frozen French fries

About 150g minced chuck steak

Salt and pepper

Beef gravy – make your own or use a packet if it's late and you're feeling lazy

A handful of diced white onions

1 tablespoon diced pickled beetroot

A few capers

A few shreds of grated horseradish

A couple of slices of dill pickle

A good squirt of French's mustard

Cook the French fries, following the pack instructions if you can read them!

Meanwhile, using your hands, form the meat into a burger patty. Season with salt and pepper and fry in a very hot heavy-bottomed frying pan – the rarer, the better.

Drain the French fries and arrange on a plate.

Cover the fries with gravy and top with the cooked burger patty.

Sprinkle the onions, beetroot, capers, horseradish and pickles over the top.

Squeeze mustard over the whole lot.

Consume.

Hang head in shame and pass out wearing your clothes, vowing never to touch alcohol ever again.

# DEAD ELVIS

This is one of The Meatwagon's only desserts. Yianni uses 7UP to make the batter because he decided it was too healthy with regular batter – 'If you're on a diet, move along – there's nothing for you here.'

## Serves 1

Oil, for deep-frying

Peanut butter, crunchy or smooth – it's your choice

White bread – you want something like Mother's Pride or Kingsmill, preferably medium sliced

Jam – the cheap, jelly-like stuff works really well here

Plain flour

7UP or similar – full fat, NOT diet

Icing sugar, for dusting (optional)

Preheat the oil to 170°C.

Spread the peanut butter on one slice of bread. Spread the jam on the other slice of bread. Bring together the two slices to form a sandwich. Stick the sandwich in the freezer for a little while to firm it up.

Meanwhile, mix the flour and 7UP into a smooth batter. It should be a bit thicker than pancake batter.

Remove the sandwich from the freezer and cut into 4 triangles. Dip each triangle in the batter and put them straight into the hot oil.

If you're cooking more than one sandwich, fry in batches according to the size of your pan or fryer. Overcrowd the sandwiches and they'll stick together. Deep-fry until golden brown. Remove from the oil and drain on kitchen paper.

Let them cool down for a few minutes before you tuck in: the filling's like peanut-flavoured magma when you first get them out of the fryer.

Dust with icing sugar and serve with vanilla ice cream. Or forget all that and just eat them straight from the kitchen counter.

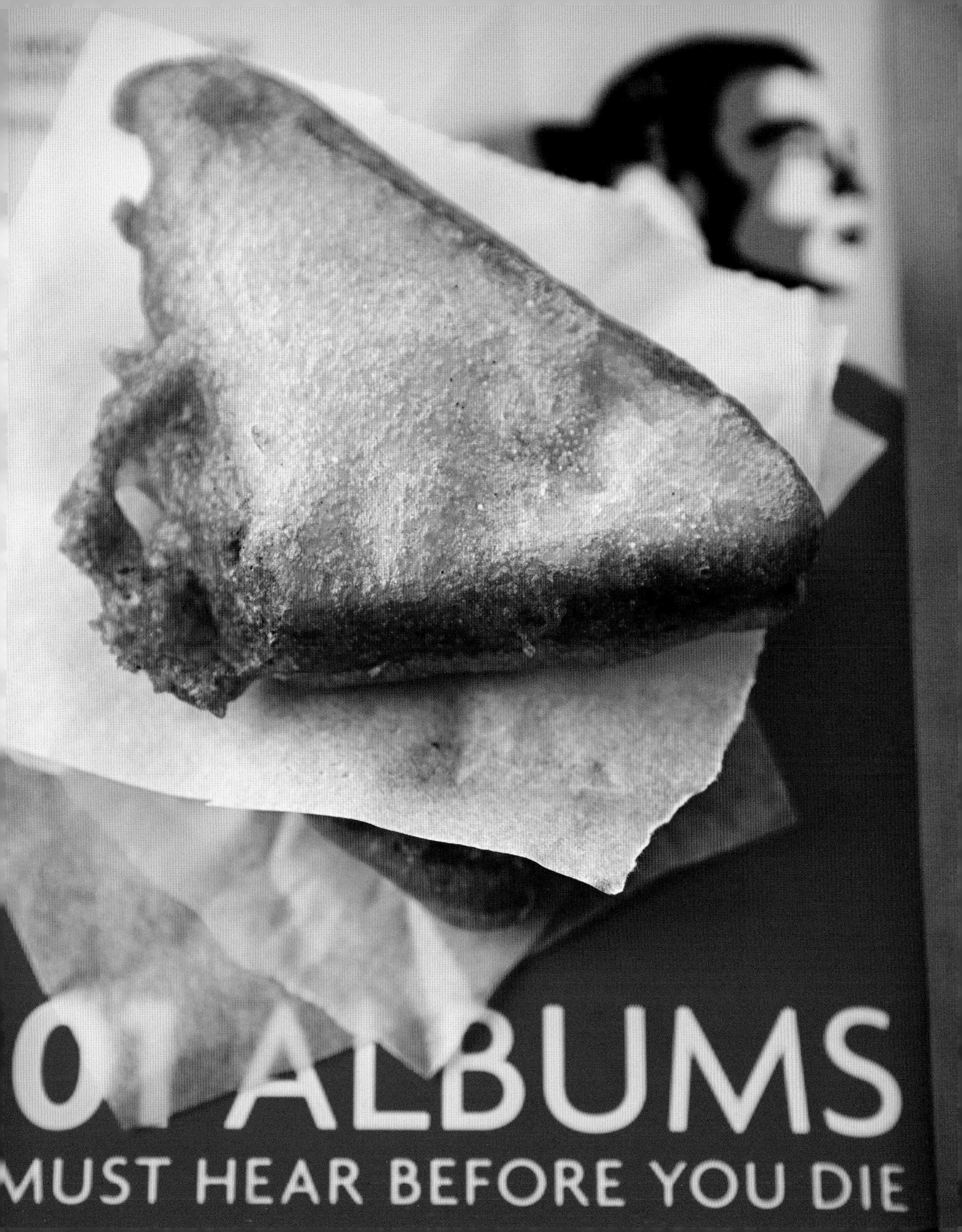

01 ALBUMS
MUST HEAR BEFORE YOU DIE

# MEAT

## Rocket & Relish
## Street Kitchen

There is something about the Airstream's aluminum, rust-proof skin. Its clean, sleek lines lend it a look of the past – and the future. Its monocoque body shell is still turning heads, 75 years after it was first launched. President Kennedy used one as a mobile office, and astronauts Neil Armstrong, Buzz Aldrin and Michael Collins were quarantined in one for three weeks in 1969 after making 'one small step for man, one giant leap for mankind'. The Airstream comes with a pedigree. That's just one of the reasons why Chris Boyd from Rocket & Relish wanted one.

'We were making hamburgers at the time,' he says. 'And the Airstream just had the the whole American hamburger/diner feel, so I decided to buy one. I took it, as a shell, to my steel people. They had fitted out catering trailers before, but nothing like an Airstream. They were looking at me, shaking their heads, saying, "You'll have

trouble getting the equipment in, because the doors are quite small. And you can't put square fridges into round corners." They were saying it couldn't be done. But I was saying it could.'

Everything had to be custom-made. Everything. From the work-tops to the extraction. And Chris admits that he had no idea quite how much the whole thing would end up costing. 'They're a very sturdy caravan, but once you've put in two tons of catering equipment, the floor has to be strengthened. I've just added a new fibreglass floor so that I can pour boiling water onto it and it will self-clean. But no matter what trailer I bought I would have wanted to make changes. Even if I bought a white chippy van. But, as it is, I bought the best.'

Chris is not the typical 'get your motor running, head out on the highway' type of mobiler. Quite the opposite, in fact. Life on the road is – for Chris – the worst part of the job.

# Cooking on the streets is a very different discipline.

'For an event,' he says, 'you've got to move all your fridge vans, trailers and staff on site. You might think, "Fantastic – a music festival for three days." But you could be there for eight or nine days getting your pitch, setting up, and going through gas checks, food hygiene checks, fire checks and all the other checks. It's a headache.'

But it's a headache he doesn't want to get rid of. He likes the adrenaline of selling food on the street. Just turning up – and doing it. 'When you're doing an event,' says Chris, 'you've got up to 100,000 people as your customer base. You've got three days to get recognition and sell your product. It's a buzz. With fixed premises, it's seven days a week and it takes much longer for people to recognise you. It's a long drag to get there. And you're not going to do the volume. It's still a buzz, but the buzz is more elongated.'

He makes money. But not silly money – not the £10,000 a day, cash in hand, that some mobilers can turn over. 'There are people out there who can do that,' says Chris. 'Like the guys who sell stews at Glastonbury. Straight into a pot. Or, in the old days, the guys who were deep-frying burgers and banging them out. We're not high enough volume to take that kind of money. Even if we're working 14 hours a day.' In order to capitalise on his expertise, Chris decided to move into bricks and mortar. Yianni of The Meatwagon tried it with MeatEasy and it seemed to offer possibilities.

Rents at the big events had been on the increase. 'At two events I can think of, we didn't even cover the rent – never mind our food costs and staff costs,' he says. 'No two years are ever exactly the same. They change the entrance or change the exit and the whole thing's thrown off. Every time you go out it's a gamble. If the gamble pays off, great. But if it doesn't, four times in a row, suddenly it's: "Woah!"' 'The new Rocket & Relish restaurant is now doing great business, but Chris won't get rid of the Airstream: 'It would be like losing my right arm.'

Jun Tanaka has done it all in reverse. He's got the restaurant doing great business – Pearl, in London. But now he's bought an Airstream and moved into street food. Jun is just the latest big-name chef to take his 'brand' out to a new audience. Jamie Oliver has got his retro ice cream van, parked up outside Jamie's Italian in London. Tom Colicchio – the face of tv's *Top Chef* – is rolling out his sandwich carts to San Francisco and Las Vegas. And restaurateur Danny Meyer is cooking up his hot dogs and shakes in the middle of a New York park. Clearly, there's money in street food.

But cooking on the streets is a very different discipline. 'If you're working in a professional kitchen, the only limitation is you,' says Jun. 'And your creativity. In a truck you're limited by everything else. In my restaurant, if I'm trying out a new dish, I don't think: "Well, I've only got a certain number of chefs and they won't be able to cope with anything too complicated." Or, "I don't have the right equipment to make this dish work." I just think about creating the best flavour. When I'm working on the street, I just have to do the best I can.'

Jun, and his partner Mark Jankel, launched Street Kitchen during the 2010 London Restaurant Festival. It was high concept. 'We were very clear about our ethos from the start – it was all about sourcing everything from great farms within the UK. But because we wanted the food to be accessible to everyone, we had in our mind a price point that we couldn't go over. We had seen people in London prepared to pay £6 for a burrito or a gourmet burger. So we decided to set our top price at £6.50. That seemed fair.'

On a trip to New York, Jun did the round of food trucks. His favourite was Schnitzel & Things,

where the queues regularly snake round the block. He thought their lightly breaded cutlets of chicken, pork and cod were fried to golden perfection, but awkward to eat. 'I got a big platter, a knife and fork and a huge deep-fried schnitzel, and I needed a table to put it on. I just grabbed mine in my hand and ate it like a sandwich. Street food should be easy to eat – I think they had forgotten that at Schnitzel & Things.'

With Street Kitchen, Jun wanted people to be able to hold their bowl in one hand and their cutlery in the other. 'And I didn't want the food to feel too cheffy. At Pearl, people come to eat my style of cuisine. They're already foodies, and they're coming to experience what I want to put on the plate. But street food is different. It's all about catering to absolutely everybody. If someone comes up and sees a fancy-sounding dish on the menu, and it doesn't connect with them immediately, you've lost their custom forever.'

To see how service should work, Jun visited Daddy Donkey Kick Ass Mexican Grill in London. The business has gone from a rickety wooden barrow to a big, bright burro-mobile by serving up to 500 people in a lunchtime. The staff of eight have to work, flat-out, in a production line. 'It's the most efficient way to do it,' says Jun. 'The customers follow the food. They order at one end, follow it along, and they pay for it at the other. The staff don't move. That's one thing we learnt very quickly. The staff have to stay in a line.'

He learnt how to manage his queue from Roland at Flaming Cactus, one of the founding fathers of the British street food movement. 'He taught us that people love to see a queue,' says Jun. 'Whether it's in front of a nightclub or a food truck. If there's a queue, people think you must be okay, so maintain your queue. When you don't have a lot of people, you slow it down a bit, and when do you have a lot of people you serve them as quickly as possible. But I've been in a restaurant kitchen for 20 years – I found it quite difficult learning to make people wait.'

Street Kitchen did a trial run in London's Covent Garden. It was an education. At the beginning, Jun and Mark were opening from 11am to 9pm. 'But one night,' says Jun, 'I saw 3,000 people leaving the Royal Opera House at 10.30pm, so we decided to open late. Two people turned up. So then we cut things back, and just did lunch. Lunch was our best time anyway. Our market was the locals who lived and worked in Covent Garden. We got regulars, who said we were a refreshing alternative to Pret. But we wasted a lot of food along the way.'

The Street Kitchen best sellers were a featherblade of organic beef from Laverstoke Park, and a fillet of hot-smoked Loch Duart salmon. The beef was braised for nine hours, at 90 degrees, before it was rolled, sliced and served with an English Pinot Noir jus. Jun introduced cheffy touches – such as a mustard dressing for the beef, and a persillade of parsley and breadcrumbs to finish it off – but he didn't bang on about them on the menu. He wanted to reach as wide an audience as possible. With 150 portions of beef and 120 portions of salmon sold every lunchtime, he clearly succeeded.

Jun now wants to set up Street Kitchens in every city in the UK. But they won't be working out of Airstreams. 'The Airstream was a mistake,' he says. 'An Airstream needs a three-ton vehicle to pull it. When you arrive, you need to level it and stabilise it. And packing it up afterwards takes ages. I think that, to be operationally efficient, you need to be able to drive your own truck – in a truck, you arrive 10 minutes before you open up. An Airstream might look beautiful, but it's just not practical. Not for me, anyway…'

# SIMPLE LAMB CASSEROLE

Casseroles always taste better the day after they're cooked. But this casserole won't be around that long – it tastes great on the day you make it. When buying meat for a casserole, Jun of Street Kitchen advises buying something with fat on as this will prevent the meat from becoming too dry.

**Serves 4**

50ml vegetable oil

Salt and pepper

800g lamb neck fillets, cut into 4cm pieces

12 button onions

4 medium carrots, thickly sliced

300ml white wine

4 garlic cloves

3 plum tomatoes, roughly chopped

1 thyme or rosemary sprig

800ml lamb stock

Handful of mint, chopped

Preheat the oven to 180°C/gas mark 4.

Heat half the vegetable oil in a frying pan. Season the lamb pieces, add to the pan and fry for 5 minutes until caramelised all over.

While the lamb is cooking, heat the remaining oil in a separate flameproof casserole and fry the button onions and carrots for 3–4 minutes, until browned.

Drain the lamb in a colander. Pour the white wine into the frying pan, bring to the boil, scrape off the sediment from the bottom of the pan, and add to the vegetables.

Add the lamb, garlic, tomatoes, herbs and stock to the casserole. The liquid should just cover the meat (add extra stock if it doesn't). Bring to the boil and place a circular piece of baking parchment over the lamb and vegetables. Cover with a lid and cook in the oven for 1½–2 hours or until the lamb is tender. Season to taste.

To serve, spoon into large bowls and scatter over the chopped mint.

# PARMESAN CHICKEN

Make sure that when the last of the chicken has been served out, you are the one who gets to run a hunk of bread around the empty dish. Just reading the ingredients of this Rocket & Relish recipe will get your mouth watering…

**Serves 4–6**

6 skinless boneless chicken breasts, cut into chunks

Seasoned flour

25g butter

1 tablespoon olive oil

150g Parmesan cheese, grated

2 tablespoons wholegrain mustard

300ml single cream

250ml chicken stock

Preheat the oven to 180°C/gas mark 4.

Toss the chicken chunks in seasoned flour. Heat the butter and oil in a flameproof casserole and fry the chicken pieces until golden – about 5–6 minutes.

Remove from the heat and add the cheese, mustard, cream and chicken stock. Stir well, season well and bake in the oven, uncovered, for 30 minutes.

Check the seasoning and serve with green beans and creamy mash.

# BEEF IN GUINNESS

This dish from Chris at Rocket & Relish is indulgent and comforting. The Guinness not only helps to tenderise the beef, it also gives a rich, malty flavour to this chunky stew.

**Serves 6–8**

2 tablespoons vegetable oil

1.5kg beef shin, cut into 5cm cubes

2 onions, roughly chopped

1 tablespoon plain flour

500ml Guinness

3 carrots, sliced

1 thyme sprig

1 bay leaf

1 garlic clove, crushed

1 teaspoon English mustard

Preheat the oven to 150°C/gas mark 2.

Heat the oil in a flameproof casserole and brown the beef in batches, ensuring it is well coloured all over. Transfer the browned beef to a plate as you go along.

Add the onions to the casserole and sauté for 10 minutes or until they are just coloured. Lower the heat and return the meat to the casserole. Add the flour and continue cooking and stirring for 3 minutes, add the Guinness, followed by the carrots, thyme, bay leaf, garlic and mustard. Season well and bring to a simmer.

Cover the casserole and place in the oven to cook for 1½–2 hours until the meat is tender. This is best served with buttery mash or champ.

# AUBERGINE BURGER

Like a thick portabella mushroom, there's something very substantial about an aubergine. 'It has a meaty, smoky flavour,' says Chris of Rocket & Relish, 'and is able to withstand other flavour combinations – without being overpowered.'

**Serves 1**

> 6 slices of aubergine
>
> 2 tablespoons olive oil
>
> Salt and pepper
>
> ¼ onion, sliced
>
> 1 large burger bun
>
> 1 slice of goat's cheese
>
> 6 sun-blushed tomatoes
>
> 1 tablespoon tomato relish
>
> 2 slices of tomato
>
> Handful of rocket leaves

Preheat a chargrill pan. Lightly brush the aubergine slices with olive oil. Season, then chargrill for 1–2 minutes on each side. Set to one side.

Meanwhile, fry the onion in the remaining olive oil. Split the burger bun and toast lightly. Place the aubergine on the base, followed by the fried onion, then the goat's cheese, followed by the sun-blushed tomatoes and tomato relish, tomatoes and rocket leaves. Top with the burger bun lid and enjoy.

# PIES

## Eat My Pies

There was never an Eat My Pies 'business model' – Andy Bates isn't a business model kind of fella. 'I just wanted something to do on a Sunday,' he says. 'I thought, "I'll make pies, run a stall and listen to the cricket." ' But it hasn't worked out like that – he's too busy serving the long line of customers who come from far and wide to taste his Scotch eggs, pork pies and custard tarts. By the time he's served them, England are all out. And the Australians are batting again.

Andy had always made pies. Whether it was a high day or a holiday, Andy would never turn up empty-handed. 'There's nothing like a pie,' he says. 'Especially a big pie. To make people smile. I've got friends with a bit of money in their pockets, but if I give them a pie which I've made myself, you can see how chuffed they are. The feeling lasts for a few days, and then I get a text message saying, "I've just had the last slice – thank you." I like that feeling.'

Pies are part of Britain's history – just think of all the references to pies in the nursery rhymes of our childhood. There was Simple Simon, who met that pieman, going to the fair. And Tom, Tom, the piper's son, who stole a pig and away did run. The 'pig' that he stole was actually a sweetmeat pie from a street trader. So, whether it's a sweet pie, a savoury pie, or four-and-twenty-blackbirds-baked-into-a-pie, we are pie crazy. Pies are in our very DNA.

Andy, however, didn't know what to do with his genetic predisposition towards pies. He had no formal business training. He had been to catering college, and was working – part-time – as a chef. 'But, at 30 years old, I got to thinking: "I want to run my own business." I had been speaking about setting up a pie stall for two years, and a friend just turned round to me and said, "Why don't you do it?" It was the kick start I needed. "Oh," I said. "I will." '

The early success of Andy's stalls in Brick Lane and Whitecross Street markets was down to his pastry. He knew the secret – love your pastry, and it will love you in return. From years of watching food programmes, he had learnt not to overhandle it. It just increases the gluten development. The butter is there to separate the gluten lumps – if it melts, the gluten molecules join together and you get tough pastry. That's why, when you've got pastry to make, you need to keep everything cold.

'But I started in the summer,' says Andy. 'I had a terrible time of it. I bought marble slabs and froze them at night. I would try to get into the kitchen by 6am – before the kitchen got hot – because after 8am it was no good. I was using pâte sucrée recipes from various cookbooks and, to be honest, I found them a little bit unworkable.

Andy Bates is happy to think of himself as a modern-day pieman.

The high-end chef's recipes were a little bit out of my league. So I developed my own. I think it worked.'

For his meat pies, Andy uses a hot-water crust pastry. It's a classic, old-school recipe that bakes to a rich brown, and holds in the wet pie filling very snugly. When you cut open Andy's crusts, you will be struck by the colour of what's inside. It isn't artificial. It's wholesome. And whether there's a lip of untrimmed pastry, hanging over the edge of the pie tin, or slight variations in the colouration on the top, Andy's pies all feel wonderfully hand-made.

Andy Bates is happy to think of himself as a modern-day pieman. In Victorian times, the pieman would hawk for business on the streets with a large tray of pies on top of his head – or strapped to the front of his chest. If customers

wanted a pie with sauce, they would make a hole in the top of the crust with their finger, and the pieman would pour in the gravy. Andy likes the idea. He's now developing his own range of Eat My Pies sauces and condiments.

Andy has a kitchen unit (Pieworld, as he likes to call it) and a rickshaw for deliveries – the Piemobile. A sign on its bumper says: 'There are no pies left in this vehicle overnight' – well, it warns off hungry kids in the neighbourhood. The Piemobile doesn't have to pay road tax or congestion charge. 'And I can park it on double yellow lines,' says Andy. 'The traffic wardens just stand there, scratching their heads. They're like: "We can't nick you." I say, "I know. That's why I bought it." '

Andy has recruited a top sales team – Mum and Dad. 'Well,' he says, 'they watched me struggle during my 20s, so they're as chuffed as chips to help out now. My Mum used to work demonstrating kitchens. Whenever I went to work with her, I would hear her say, "You need a new kitchen don't you, sir?" ' As a saleswoman, Andy's Mum was used to dealing with customers – and rejection. 'On the stall, I can still take it personally. But she can joke, and have someone buying a pie by the end of it.'

Now the Americans want a slice of Eat My Pies. While Andy was researching the New York street food scene, he set up shop in Brooklyn. In the middle of an eclectic mix of vintage mink stoles, broken alarm clocks and *Star Wars* collectibles, he sold out – in three hours. 'Everyone was asking for Scottish eggs. I explained that they were called Scotch eggs, and they weren't actually from Scotland. But when I sliced one in front of them, and the yolk was runny, I got lots of oohs and aahs.'

Andy wasn't very taken with what he saw of the New York street food scene. 'I wasn't blown away by anything at all,' he says. 'I found it fairly average. And the packaging? Everything came in three or four layers of plastic. I get people in London who won't buy a slice of custard tart from me because it's in a plastic box. I thought New Yorkers would be the same. But no. I think we've got the best street food in the world right now. I really do. And it's only going to get better.'

eat my pies...

# INDIVIDUAL PORK PIES

These were the first pies that Andy ever sold – on a stall in Brick Lane market. He still sells them. The sage and mustard give them a real kick.

**Makes 10**

*1 kg pork mince*

*2 tablespoons Worcestershire sauce*

*2 tablespoons English mustard (or more if you like…)*

*Large pinch of chopped fresh sage*

*1 teaspoon salt*

*Coarsely ground black pepper*

*Pinch of grated nutmeg*

For the pastry:

*450g plain flour, plus extra for dusting*

*1 teaspoon salt*

*200ml water*

*170g lard or butter*

*2 egg yolks, beaten, to glaze*

Preheat the oven to 200°C/gas mark 6.

Mix the meat thoroughly with all the other filling ingredients. Season to your liking (you'll need lots of pepper). Divide the mix into ten 100g portions. Roll into balls and refrigerate for 10–15 minutes.

Now prepare the pastry. Mix the flour and salt in a large bowl and make a well in the centre. Bring the water and lard or butter to the boil in a saucepan, then quickly stir into the flour with a wooden spoon to form a smooth dough. Leave to cool for 5 minutes.

Roll out the pastry on a floured surface to about 5mm thick. Place the 'meat balls' onto the pastry. Cut around each ball double the size, then wrap the pastry all around the filling, pinching and smoothing to create a ball. There should be no holes or gaps in the pastry.

With a 6mm cutter, cut small circles from the remaining pastry, brush with egg yolk and place one on top of each pie to create a lid.

Place the pies on greaseproof paper on a baking tray and brush all over with egg yolk for a golden finish. With a knife, make a small hole in the lid to allow steam to escape while cooking.

Bake for 35 minutes until golden and oozing in juice. Eat either hot or cold.

# PICCALILLI

Andy couldn't stand this when he was younger, but he now deems this version from Sean Lawson, Head chef of Eat My Pies, 'The perfect accompaniment to a cold raised pie, ham and cheese sandwich or salt beef roll'.

## Makes 3 x 450g jars

| | |
|---|---|
| 1 small cauliflower, cut into small florets | 400ml white wine vinegar |
| 2 medium carrots, diced into 1cm cubes | 200ml malt vinegar |
| 160g French beans, cut into 1cm pieces | 50g mustard powder |
| 1 cucumber, peeled and diced into 1cm cubes | 25g turmeric |
| | 350g caster sugar |
| 10 silverskin onions | ½ dried chilli |
| 1 can of sweetcorn, drained | 3 cardamon pods, split |
| Maldon sea salt | 3 tablespoons grain mustard |
| ½ teaspoon coriander seeds | 5 tablespoons cornflour |

Place all the vegetables in a bowl with good handful of sea salt. Leave for 1 hour, then rinse them in cold water and drain.

Meanwhile, combine the rest of the ingredients, except the cornflour, in a large pot and bring to the boil.

Whisk the cornflour with a little cold water and use it to thicken the spice mixture. Add the vegetables to the pot and cook for 4–5 minutes.

Spoon into sterilised jars and cover immediately. Once cooled, label each jar and store for up to four weeks before using to get the best flavour. It will keep for several months.

# BLACK PUDDING SCOTCH EGGS

For a different take on this recipe, Andy recommends using the Spanish Morcilla de Burgos black pudding. It's made with rice, and adds a lovely texture to the dish. Serve the Spanish version with very chilled lager, but serve the British version with Guinness or another dark stout.

**Makes 4**

4 large eggs

200g pork mince or pork sausagemeat

200g black pudding, finely chopped

Salt and freshly ground black pepper

For the coating:

75g seasoned plain flour

2 eggs, beaten

200g dried white breadcrumbs

Vegetable oil, for deep-frying

Boil the eggs in a saucepan of simmering water for 6 minutes. Drain and cool the eggs under cold running water, then shell them.

Mix the pork mince or sausagemeat with the black pudding in a large bowl. Season well with salt and pepper. Divide into four balls and flatten each one out, on a piece of clingfilm about 40cm square, into ovals about 12.5cm long and 7.5cm at the widest point.

Place each egg onto a meat oval, then pick the clingfilm square up by its corners and use it to wrap the meat around each egg. Make sure that the coating is smooth and completely covers the egg.

Roll each one in flour first, then in the beaten egg, ensuring it is coated completely, then roll in the breadcrumbs to cover thoroughly.

Heat the oil in a deep heavy-bottomed pan, until a breadcrumb sizzles and turns brown when dropped into it (170°C). Carefully place each Scotch egg into the hot oil and deep-fry for 7–8 minutes, until golden and crisp and the meat is completely cooked.

Carefully remove from the oil with a slotted spoon and drain on kitchen paper. Allow to rest for 15 minutes before serving.

# CHICKEN & HAM HOCK PIE

Andy came up with the idea of this award-winning pie after trudging around supermarkets and feeling sorry for the overcooked pies in the deli section. Using ham hock gives this pie so much more flavour than sliced ham, and cooking it on the bone produces a really good jelly. The addition of thyme and coarse black pepper helps to bring out best in this classic.

## Serves 8–10

2 large
ham hocks

1 carrot, chopped

1 celery stick,
chopped

1 medium onion,
chopped

1 tablespoon
black treacle

1 bunch of thyme,
chopped

Salt and black
pepper (medium
coarse ground)

6–8 chicken
thighs, boned and
skinned

### For the pastry

450g plain flour,
plus extra for
dusting

1 teaspoon salt

170g lard or
butter

200ml water

1 egg, beaten with
1 teaspoon water

Place the ham hocks in a large saucepan, cover with cold water and bring to the boil. Skim all scum from the surface, reduce to a simmer and add the vegetables, treacle and 1 teaspoon of thyme. Simmer for 2–3 hours, until the meat is just starting to fall off the bones.

Remove the ham hocks and any meat that has fallen away and allow to cool. Strain the stock into a clean pan. Return to the boil, reduce by one-third, then allow to cool. This will give you the jelly for the pie. Pick the meat from the ham hock, then flake it into a bowl and season with black pepper and chopped thyme, according to taste. Remember, this is a cold pie, so pepper will really bring out the flavour once the meat has rested and is chilled. Hocks can be very salty, so its unlikely you'll need to add any salt.

Next take the chicken and batter out with a rolling pin between two pieces of clingfilm. This will tenderise the meat. Chop roughly, then season with salt and pepper.

For the pastry, mix the flour and salt in a large bowl and make a well in the centre. Bring the water and lard to the boil in a pan, then quickly stir it into the flour to form a smooth dough. Leave to cool for 5 minutes.

Lightly grease a pie ring measuring 15–20cm by 8–10cm deep. Line the bottom with lightly greased greaseproof paper. Place on a baking tray lined with greaseproof paper. Preheat the oven to 180°C/gas mark 4.

Take two-thirds of the dough and form it into a ball. On a lightly floured worktop, roll it into a circle so it is large enough to line the pie ring and overlap the edge. Carefully lift the pastry into the pie ring, gently press into the corners and allow it just to hang over the edge. Roll out the remaining pastry into a circle for the lid. Cover the bottom of the pie with a layer of the ham, then a layer of chicken. Repeat until the pie is filled. Brush the pie edges with egg wash and top with the lid. Pinch the pastry edges together with your thumb and finger to crimp the pie and create a seal. Trim the edge with a knife so that no pastry hangs over the edge.

Brush the top of the pie with the beaten egg, and make a hole in the middle of the lid. Bake for 1 hour. Remove from the ring and brush the sides and top again with egg. Bake for a further 15 minutes. Remove from the oven and cool. Once the pie is cold, refrigerate for 2–3 hours.

Check around the pastry for any holes and fill them with softened butter so that the jelly doesn't escape. Take the jellied stock from the fridge, discard the layer of fat on the surface and gently reheat to melt the jelly. Pour the stock into the hole in the top of the pastry until the pie is filled. Chill in the fridge for 2–3 hours until the jelly is set.

# CUSTARD TART

Just about as British as it gets, with a lovely sweet pastry. Plan to make meringues the same day that you make this tart, to use up all the egg whites!

**Serves 10**

12 egg yolks (or use 5 medium eggs)

110g caster sugar

600ml double cream

Freshly grated nutmeg

For the pastry

250g plain flour, plus extra for dusting

Pinch of salt

75g icing sugar

150g chilled butter, cut into pieces

1 egg, beaten

First make the pastry. Sift the flour, salt and sugar together, then rub in the butter until the mixture resembles breadcrumbs. Slowly add the beaten egg, mixing until the pastry forms a ball. Wrap tightly in clingfilm and refrigerate for 2 hours.

Preheat the oven to 170°C/gas mark 3.

Roll out the pastry on a lightly floured surface to 2mm thickness. Use to line a deep-sided 28cm tart ring placed on a baking sheet. Rest the lined tart ring in the fridge for 20 minutes.

Line the tart ring with greaseproof paper and fill with baking beans or crumpled foil to keep the base's shape. Bake blind (i.e. without a filling) for about 20 minutes. Remove the greaseproof paper and baking beans or foil and return to the oven for 5–8 minutes or until the pastry is starting to turn golden brown. Remove from the oven and brush with egg yolk. Allow to cool.

Turn the oven down to 130°C/gas mark 1.

For the filling, whisk together the egg yolks and sugar. Add the cream and mix well, allowing a few minutes for the sugar to dissolve. Pass the mixture through a fine sieve into a large jug.

Fill the pastry case with the custard. Carefully place in the middle of the oven and bake for 30–40 minutes or until the custard appears set but not too firm. Remove from the oven and sprinkle with grated nutmeg.

Allow to cool to room temperature before serving.

# FISH

## The Fish Hut

Southwold is an old-fashioned English seaside town with elegant, Victorian Christmas card shop-fronts. Old weather-boarded fishermen's cottages, painted the colours of sugared almonds, look out over rust-stained fishing boats. It's ridiculously picturesque. Which is why the DFLs (or Down From Londons) have moved in. And it's why, during the week, Southwold is so quiet. As a sign in one of the local shops puts it, 'This is the only mortuary in the country with a bus service running through it.'

But there is life in Southwold. You just have to know where to look. Blackshore, for instance – the busy, working wharf on an unmade track that runs between Southwold and Walberswick, where the smell of tar mingles with fresh fish. The dock was first built in 1783, when it was home to Suffolk's white herring fleet. It's more genteel now. But at the end of the track, parked outside The Harbour Inn, is a little fish and chip van called The Fish Hut. And there's nothing genteel about The Fish Hut.

The Fish Hut is bold and brassy – and comes with its own seagull and sandpit. The owner, Nick Attfield, has even installed a fish tank. With plastic fish. 'It's at kid height,' he says, 'so that they can point, and go, "I want that one." The area around Southwold is famous for seagulls swooping down and eating your fish and chips as you sit on the beach. Ours are on sticks. Much safer. People like to buy a wooden seagull when they're here on holiday. Then they take it home and stick it in the loo and say, "That's from our holiday in Southwold." People like our seaside tat.'

The Fish Hut is Nick's business card. It's there to advertise his pub – The Harbour Inn. The pub is still a newish venture and, at the moment, it needs advertising. 'The Harbour Inn had a reputation for frozen everything,' he says. 'And that included the very, very expensive fish and

chips. But there's a rule in this business – never take on somewhere that's at its peak. The kitchen is tidy now. And the pub is looking nice. But we are still rated 14th out of 16 for restaurants in Southwold on the Trip Advisor website. The only way is up.'

Because it's not the mainstay of his business, Nick can be choosy about where he takes The Fish Hut. 'I'm not going to drive to Scotland to do a christening, for instance. But I did do a christening for 80 people nearby – people who use the pub. Their driveway was too steep, and I thought, "I can't get my fryers up there." So I had to do it half on the main road, half on the driveway. Tractors kept coming past me. I'm not really sure I should have had my gas cylinders on a main road, but it was a great party.'

He will travel, however, for an A-list party – The Fish Hut is now a mainstay of the celebrity circuit. Nick catered Tracy McLeod's 50th birthday. That's Tracy McLeod, the esteemed restaurant critic at the *Independent*. And they catered Piers Morgan's wedding. 'We turned up at this Sussex mansion, and there was a stunning marquee with a wonderful lady making sushi, and a whole lamb and a whole pig on a rotisserie. And then there was me and my silly little Fish Hut. But they loved it. They absolutely loved it. It's that kitsch thing again. They laughed. They got it.

Nick's best customers are Richard Curtis, the writer of *Four Weddings and a Funeral*, and his partner Emma Freud. Working for them, luckily, doesn't involve a long haul around the M25. 'They live over there,' says Nick, pointing across the water to Walberswick – Notting-Hill-on-Sea, as it's known locally. 'We did a party for Emma down on the beach at Southwold. We went out onto the pier, and set it up opposite her beach hut – all beautifully lit. We had twinkly lights, and candles, all over the beach. Great fun.'

# Nick served crab cakes, and a lobster ravioli with pasta made fresh to order.

Nick has always had a sense of style. He ran the wine society at university, and went on to become the assistant wine buyer at Harrods. But he soon realised he would rather work on the restaurant floor than the shop floor. So he took a job as front of house manager at The Bell in Walberswick. 'But I've always been of the opinion that you need to know exactly how everything works so that you can tell the other guys what to do. I realised that the kitchen is the place where you make your money – and the kitchen is where you employ your idiots. So I ended up there more and more often.'

One day – one seminal day – chef was sick. It was a busy Sunday lunch. So Nick did the right thing. 'I got everything out of the fridge, and stuck it on the table in front of me. I worked out what I could cook and, basically, it was everything with new potatoes and salad. I made the front of house guy tell everyone: "I don't know how long the food will take, but you will get served – come hell or high water." We did 90 lunches. Once your boss sees you can do it, you don't get out. And once you realise you can do it, you don't want to get out. My future was decided.'

He had big ideas. For the local food festival, he decided to drag his kitchen onto the beach at Aldeburgh. 'I had seen tv chefs doing it,' he says. 'So I thought: "Why not?" He served crab cakes, and a lobster ravioli with pasta made fresh

to order. 'The sun shone and we won lots of customers for the pub,' he says. 'The year after, the festival organisers said, "Just do fish and chips." I knew I couldn't have a trestle table with deep fat fryers on if I had 300 people standing in front of me. So I had to think of a way of doing it safely.'

He thought 'trailer'. And began his search with Ebay. 'I typed in "fish and chip trailer" and saw these ugly great things that cost a fortune. Then I thought about a doughnut trailer. I never wanted to trade at Glastonbury, or do a huge number of covers. So I didn't need anything big. We found a little doughnut trailer that was doing car-boot sales near Lowestoft. A couple of friends helped me decorate it in a field. And another friend made the roof.' The Fish Hut was born.

Nick still can't stand up in the hut – he has to hold his head to one side when he's frying. But it makes him look interested in the wellbeing of his customers. Otherwise, size isn't an issue. 'At Harrods,' he says, 'they had chefs working in cupboards because retail space was so precious. When we did a kitchen extension at The Bell, we had to crane in a mobile kitchen. I thought we would have to slim down the menu, but we just adapted. It's amazing what you can do in a tiny kitchen. All that happened when we moved into our massive new kitchen was that we just made more mess in more corners.'

Given its location on the Suffolk coast, it makes sense that The Fish Hut specialises in fish and chips. But which fish? There are regional variations in our national dish. Roughly speaking, it's cod in the south, skate in the Midlands, and

The fish Hut

haddock in the north. But, despite the scares about overfishing, Nick is happiest using cod. 'I use the local day boats which work within very strict quotas,' he says. 'If they are catching cod through long lining, then I reckon it's perfectly all right for me to use it.' And the clean white curds of fish work perfectly with Nick's freshly minted mushy peas.

'I have tried other fish,' he says. 'Pollock, coley and whiting, for instance. They're all right on day one, or day two. But they deteriorate very quickly. And I won't use anything from the trawlers that come down from Lowestoft, or up from Essex, which, when these poor blokes don't get their quotas, come and hoover up everything off the seabed. The guys in Blackshore are so tightly controlled, and I believe they can fish sustainably. I want to support them as best I can. I grew up round here, and I feel like I owe it to them.'

Blackshore is in the process of getting funding from Europe to improve facilities for the local fishermen. Reinforcing the harbour – that sort of thing. But it won't stretch to resurfacing the road. 'The road is part of Blackshore's charm,' says Nick. Despite the potholes, the quay is thriving. Three or four years ago, there was only one full-time fisherman, with hobbyists catching herring, cod and sea bass. Now there are eight fishermen. And they're expanding their catch to include shellfish. 'That's the best thing about working here,' says Nick. 'The produce.'

The Fish Hut isn't restricted to fish and chips. It's adaptable. The fryers can come out, and stoves can go in. It's just a shell. A lovely, inspired shell. But fish and chips are a great way to feed people at a party. And feeding all sorts of demographics – if you're 5 or 105, you love fish and chips. 'It's roughly the same price as a hog roast,' says Nick, ever the salesman. 'But it's not a hog roast – which everyone's done to death.' However, there's something else about The Fish Hut. Something special. It makes people smile.

'I love working in the Fish Hut,' says Nick. 'At the pub, people are already my captive audience. I can say, "Try this wine", or "We've got rock eel on the menu – why don't you give it a go?" But The Fish Hut is like a sales pitch. Because it takes a little while to cook your fish and chips, we try and explain why we're there. We get to talk properly to people. And then we invite them to come down to the pub. I like that element of it. I always have business cards. Even at the British Street Food Awards, in Ludlow, it was amazing how many cards we handed out.'

He's now got a taste for working on the street, and has set his heart on a wood-fired pizza oven – bolted onto a Vespa Ape. Of course, the Ape wouldn't be able to move anywhere, once it was weighed down with the oven. But Nick has thought of that. He'll put it on a low-loader. He has already got the oven – it's sitting in a nearby barn. 'Now we just need the Ape. But, because we're going to chop it up, it would make sense for us to find one that's been involved in some kind of accident. Watch this space.'

# PERFECT FISH & CHIPS

Nick uses the fat 'whale cod' fillets for his perfect fish and chips. They come from the 'thick' end of the cod (Nick isn't a fisherman, so he cannot be more anatomically correct), so you get the gloriously plump white segments of fish and can eat all the crispy batter without fear of bone or slimy skin. But nothing gets wasted. 'The thin end of the fish end up in our fish pie,' says Nick, 'and the bony bit and the belly fat are used to make stock.'

## Serves 6

2 pints of lager
(1.2 litres)

Plain flour – about
500g

1 teaspoon Bird's
custard powder

12 potatoes (not
new potatoes), cut
into chips of equal
thickness

Sea salt and pepper

Oil, for deep-frying
(anything but
olive oil)

6 x 150g cod or
haddock fillets

For the mushy peas:

1kg bag of frozen
peas

300ml double cream

4 garlic cloves, finely
chopped

2 vegetable stock
cubes

1 large bunch of
mint leaves, stalks
removed

To make the batter, place the lager in a bowl and slowly whisk in the flour until you can draw a figure of 8 in the mixture with the top of the 8 disappearing by the time you have reached the top again. Whisk in the custard powder, which gives colour and flavour, and leave to rest in the fridge for 30 minutes.

For the chips, Nick's preferred method is to blanch them in water. This means the chips contain less saturated fat and are much more fluffy in the middle. Have a bucket of iced water ready and a pan of sea-salted water, which has been brought to the boil. Cook your chips, two handfuls at a time, in the pan of water until they are just cooked and immediately scoop them out with a spider or slotted spoon into the iced water. Drain your potatoes in a colander until the water has gone (NEVER PUT THEM INTO A FRYER IMMEDIATELY AFTER BOILING THEM!). Heat your fryer to 180°C and cook the chips until crisp and golden. Remove them from the oil and drain on kitchen paper. Keep them warm while you fry the fish.

Pat the fish fillets dry with kitchen paper, then dip them into the batter. Carefully lower into the deep-fat fryer, one or two at a time, and fry for 3–4 minutes, until golden brown. Drain on kitchen paper.

For the mushy peas, bring a pan of salted water to the boil. Add the peas, cook for 3 minutes, and refresh immediately in cold or iced water. Meanwhile, put the cream, garlic and stock cubes in a pan, bring to a simmer and leave to infuse for 10 minutes.

Drain the peas and place in a food processor with the cream mixture and mint. Blitz until it resembles a coarse paste. Season to taste and serve with the fish and chips.

# BOUILLABAISSE

Nick likes to think of this as a French classic, with a Suffolk twist. He uses this recipe as a base and adds bits of fish from the local boats – in Suffolk there's plenty of rock eel, cod, mackerel and skate wings. They can be cut up into pieces and poached in the stock at the last moment.

## Serves 6–8

1kg soup tomatoes (or soft over-ripe tomatoes)

500g–1kg shellfish shells, preferably langoustine or lobster (you could use the crab shells from the crab cake recipe on page 98)

3 large Spanish onions, diced

1 garlic bulb, diced

Knob of butter

3 leeks, sliced

3 large carrots, diced

1 celery head, roughly chopped

1 fennel bulb, sliced

1 tablespoon tomato purée

1 litre clear fish stock

1 bunch of curly parsley, leaves picked and finely chopped and stalks reserved

3 bay leaves

3 generous glugs of Pernod

Salt, pepper and sugar

Preheat the oven to 200°C/gas mark 6.

Put the tomatoes into a baking tray and roast them in the oven until they start to melt and their edges are a deep red – about 20–30 minutes.

Put the shells in another baking tray and roast in the oven for about 10 minutes until they start to become lighter in colour (you will be able to smell the flavour being released slowly). Set aside.

Next sweat the onions and garlic in a saucepan with the butter until they start to caramelise. Add the leeks, carrots, celery and fennel and cook until they begin to soften. Stir the tomato purée into the vegetables and then add the roasted tomatoes and shells.

Smash the shells in the pan with a wooden spoon, stirring all the time. This helps to release the flavour. Add the fish stock to the mixture, along with the parsley stalks and bay leaves. (If it seems as though the mixture needs more liquid, add a little water until you reach a soup-like consistency.) Bring to a simmer and cook for around 40–45 minutes.

Remove the shellfish stock from the heat and strain through a sieve into another pan. Be sure to squeeze as much liquid from the vegetables as possible.

Add the Pernod and parsley leaves to the stock and season with salt, pepper and a little sugar.

# CRAB CAKES

Freshly cooked and dressed crabs are widely available from about Easter onwards at Aldeburgh. Nick scoops out the meat and returns the shell to the fisherman – who then uses it again…

**Serves 6**

> 500g potatoes, cut into even pieces
>
> 125g butter
>
> 1 bunch of spring onions, finely chopped
>
> 2 garlic cloves
>
> 3 green chillies, diced
>
> 50g fresh ginger, peeled and grated
>
> 1 tablespoon ground cumin
>
> 4 large crabs, cooked and dressed
>
> Juice of 1 lime
>
> 1 bunch of fresh coriander, chopped
>
> 6 eggs
>
> Plain flour
>
> ½ loaf of white bread, turned into breadcrumbs
>
> Salt and freshly ground pepper
>
> Vegetable oil, for frying

Place the potatoes in a pan of boiling water and cook until they are soft. Mash them with half the butter and set aside.

Put the remaining butter in a pan on top of the stove. Add the spring onions, garlic, chillies and ginger and sweat them off without colouring them. Then add the cumin and remove from the heat.

Scrape the crabmeat out of the shells into a large bowl and mash with a fork. Add the potato, onion mixture, lime juice and coriander and stir until well combined. Place in the fridge for 30 minutes to cool.

Meanwhile, whisk the eggs in a bowl until they resemble an egg wash. Put the flour and breadcrumbs into separate bowls.

Remove the crab mixture from the fridge and season to taste with salt and pepper. Form into round cakes 5cm wide by 2cm thick. Next, flour, egg and breadcrumb the cakes. Cover and place in the fridge.

When you are ready to serve, heat a little oil in a frying pan and cook and turn the cakes until golden brown and hot in the middle. Alternatively, deep-fry them for 3–4 minutes.

Serve with mixed leaves and sweet chilli sauce.

# LOBSTER RAVIOLI

If you're tight (or cooking commercially), add some poached salmon to bulk out the meat. But otherwise, just go for it. The Dow's up.

**Serves 4**

*200g '00' flour*

*2 medium eggs*

*Olive oil*

**Generous pinch of saffron strands (optional)**

**For the lobster filling:**

*1 medium live lobster*

*100g poached salmon (optional)*

*3–4 tablespoons double cream*

*Salt and freshly ground pepper*

*2 tablespoons finely chopped fresh herbs (such as dill or parsley)*

*Lemon juice*

*1 egg, beaten*

To make the pasta, put the flour and and eggs into a food processor and blitz into pea-sized clumps, adding tiny amounts of water and olive oil to get the right consistency. To make it extra special, prepare a saffron tea by infusing a generous pinch of saffron strands in a little boiling water and add this to the dough mixture to give a more golden final pasta. Transfer to a lightly floured surface and knead into a ball. Wrap in clingfilm and rest in the fridge for at least 20 minutes.

Put your live lobster in the freezer to make it feel sleepy humanely. Then plunge into a very large saucepan of boiling water and slam on the lid. Our medium-sized lobsters take about 20 minutes. Allow to cool, then crack open every bit of shell to extract all the meat. Keep the shells to roast for your next batch of fish stock.

Gently blitz the meat (and the salmon, if using) with a little cream, seasoning, fresh herbs and lemon juice. Taste to check the seasoning.

Use a pasta machine to roll out sheets of pasta and lay onto a worktop. Place teaspoonful dollops of lobster mixture on top, well-spaced. Place a pasta sheet on top, and use a cutter to make your round ravioli, sealed with egg wash. Poach in salted boiling water for about 3 minutes – no longer. Serve as simply as possible.

# SUNDAY LUNCH

# The Bridge Inn

On the *Pride of Belhaven*, there is always a safety demonstration. No 'cabin doors to manual and cross check', you understand. Just Hamish, the skipper, pointing out the two small exits on the canal boat as he pulls away from the towpath. Hamish prides himself on the fact that his Sunday lunch cruise is a relaxed affair. For a start, he won't be travelling above 3mph. And he knows that if anything does goes wrong, it won't be serious – the Union Canal, just outside Edinburgh, is only four feet deep. The diners would hardly get their feet wet.

But accidents do happen – even at 3mph. Hamish will, for instance, be navigating the *Pride of Belhaven* over a narrow aqueduct. 'It's 62 foot of boat, with a clearance of only a few inches on either side,' he says, 'and if you approach the aqueduct at the wrong angle, you'll get quite a bang. Around here it's easy to get a piece of wood caught between your rudder and your rudder stem – and your steering suddenly goes. All you can do is slam the boat into

reverse, and bang into the bank. You do have to be careful.'

The *Pride of Belhaven* is moored outside the Bridge Inn, in the pretty village of Ratho – eight miles outside Edinburgh. The inn was a farmhouse, built in the middle of the 18th century, and was compulsorily purchased for the building of the Union Canal. It became a staging post, offering travellers food and accommodation – an early version of a motorway service station. But with cleaner toilets. When Rachel and Graham Bucknall took over the inn, in 2010, the *Pride of Belhaven* came as part of the deal. As they say, it's been an education.

Having worked at Justin de Blank, the Belgravia eaterie, Rachel had hands-on food experience – she was in charge of all the cooked food for the Harvey Nichols Food Hall. But she had no experience of boats. 'Well,' she says, 'we had a little boat that the family used to fish for mackerel – in Fife. We took our lobster pots down with us, and had a lovely time.' But the *Pride of Belhaven*

was different. Bigger, for a start. 'Thank heavens that Hamish, the skipper, came with the business. At least he knew what he was doing.'

Rachel started by putting her pork on the menu. She ran a farm on the other side of the canal from the Bridge Inn, and decided to up the breeding programme to supply the boat. She crossed Willow, her prize Saddleback, with a Black. 'Saddlebacks give lovely crackling,' she says, 'but they can get a bit too fat. So I got a Black in to see if the piglets would be a bit leaner.' They were. Head chef Lee Skelton is happy to put a slower-maturing meat on his menu because when the pigs reach the right level of 'finish', they have developed a lot more flavour.

Lee is frantically trying to cook up a three-course lunch – including sea bream, and Rachel's pork – in the bowels of the boat. His cookers

aren't mounted in gimbals. His chopping boards aren't clamped onto the work surfaces. And his knives aren't held tightly to the walls by magnetic strips. He doesn't feel the need. Hamish has been skippering for 10 years now, and Lee is confident in his abilities. To be fair, it must calm the nerves when you can see families with young children on the towpath who are travelling faster than you are.

Today, Lee has to prep 20 covers. He can work miracles with a four-burner stove, a bain-marie and a 'hot cupboard' – anyway, a traditional gas oven would use far too much gas. It doesn't make things any easier that Lee is working with a new kitchen assistant – the last one suffered from seasickness. 'I'll do my best,' he says. 'I've learnt to adapt my menu to the boat. Which means I've got cold starters, to free the top of the stove for main courses like my pan-fried sea bream. On a boat it's all got to be quick and easy.'

The water looks calm. But the fire extinguishers in the boat's kitchen are still strapped down – just in case. And there's a guard on the stove, to stop the pots flying off. 'Unfortunately,' says Lee, 'that means I have to tuck my frying pan handle between the bars. In the last really bad gale, the wind was so powerful that we got blown around and the plates crashed onto the floor. And once I was flaming a strawberry for dessert when Hamish banged the boat against the side. I was lucky I didn't lose my finger.'

Hildur, the waitress, brings round the wine list – there are no licensing restrictions once the *Pride of Belhaven* is underway. 'We could serve 24 hours a day if we wanted to,' says Rachel. 'We had a lot of Frenchmen over for a France *v.* Scotland match, and they all turned up at 12pm. Our licensing in the pub doesn't start until 12.30pm, so we thought, "What on earth do you do with 30 Frenchmen, desperate for beer?" We put them in the boat, pootled off down the canal, played them some Scottish music, and served them beer. It was lovely.'

To think that the railways nearly killed off Britain's canals. People thought of them as little more than foul-smelling ditches, and they faced a future of abandonment and closure. In the 1950s, all that was left was a handful of boats, struggling through a dirty and decaying system. It took a group of forward-thinking individuals – the Inland Waterways Association – to persuade the government to recognise the potential of the canal system for leisure and tourism and, in 1968, the Transport Act stopped the rot.

There are now three times more boats using the network than there were in 1968 – enough traffic to warrant the opening of the Millennium Ribble Link at Preston, the first new canal in a

# To think that the railways nearly killed off Britain's canals.

century. And all over Britain, people are starting to discover the joy of eating and drinking on the water. There is a new network of cafés and restaurant boats, including the *Glassboat* in Bristol, the *Gongoozler's Rest* in Braunston and the *Oliver Cromwell* in Gloucester Docks. There are coffee boats and ice cream boats – even cheese boats, with spontaneous cheese tastings along the towpath.

And it's not just the canals. It's our rivers as well. *The Visitor Boat*, for instance, is a converted coal barge on the Thames where waiters garnish the food with herbs, fresh from the 'garden' – upstairs, on the deck of the boat. Diners can hear the waves beneath them. They can see the majesty of Tower Bridge through the windows. And they can smell the tug-boat diesel as it's blown along from Westminster pier. But with a roster of magnificent chefs to draw on, it's not the smell of diesel that the diners take away with them.

Ten years ago, the Union Canal was classed as a 'remainder waterway' – part of it had been filled in. But in a flurry of activity around the Millennium, the funding was found to renovate it. Diners can now travel from Edinburgh to Falkirk by canal. While they eat, they can watch the swans, the herons, the stoats and the otters. And the optimistic fishermen. Hamish remembers watching a Frenchman pull out a pike. 'I wouldn't have eaten it – but he marinated it in red wine overnight and ate it the next day for his lunch. He loved it.'

Lee – who likes to fish on his days off – has never put pike on the menu. He doesn't need to. He has access to top-quality local produce. Whether it's Rachel's pork, stuffed with haggis, or pheasant from a local gamekeeper served up with apples from Rachel's orchard. And if ever he's in danger of running out – and can't convince enough people on board to switch their order – Rachel will just hop into the 4 x 4 and drive extra supplies down to him. 'Many is the time that she's jumped on the boat with a whole blackcurrant cheesecake.'

Hamish is still up on deck – focused on the canal as it winds ahead. He keeps looking at his watch because he's intent on running the *Pride of Belhaven* to time. He knows that Lee likes to serve the diners their starters and main courses on the way to the aqueduct – and their desserts and coffee on the way back. 'But if the chef's had a bit of a bad night, he might not get the food out as quickly as usual,' says Hamish. 'So I've got to find a way of slowing things down.' Which would, effectively, mean going backwards.

After a brief stop at the aqueduct, Hamish turns the boat round. And Hildur serves up dessert – from a distance. 'You have to be careful,' she says. 'Normally, customers will reach out. But I don't go too near them, in case there's a little accident.' Charlie, her assistant, knows all about little accidents. He has just spilt red wine on the white tablecloth. 'He was shaking,' says Hildur. 'He wouldn't take the desserts out at all. He left that to me. Normally I put a little doily underneath the bowls, so they don't slip. But he'll learn in time.'

# PORK BELLY STUFFED WITH HAGGIS

Folk on the *Pride of Belhaven* like a bit of Scottish fayre, so Lee came up with the idea of adding haggis to the pork belly. Hamish likes to point out the pigs as the diners cruise past Rachel's farm.

### Serves 8–10

2kg pork belly (ask your butcher to remove the ribs)

700g haggis, removed from outer casing

Sea salt and pepper

100g butter

2 shallots, finely diced

2 garlic cloves, finely diced

500g wild mushrooms, sliced

1 small bunch of thyme, chopped

100ml brandy

500ml double cream

500ml beef stock

Preheat the oven to 220°C/gas mark 7.

Score the pork belly skin in quite narrow lines, using a very sharp kitchen or craft knife. Lie it flat on a board, skin side down. Stuff the centre with haggis, then roll up and tie tightly with butcher's twine. Season the skin with sea salt. Roast in the oven for 15 minutes to crisp the skin, then turn the oven down to 180°C/gas mark 4 and roast for 30 minutes per 500g (i.e. 1 hour for a 1kg piece). Allow the meat to rest for 20 minutes before slicing and serving. This also works well made the day before, then sliced while cold. To reheat, place the slices in the oven on a baking tray for about 20 minutes. If you would like the haggis slightly crispy, put the slices under the grill before serving. This makes it ideal for a dinner party because it can be prepared well in advance.

To make the cream sauce to accompany the pork, melt the butter in a large saucepan and add the shallots and garlic. Sweat in a pan for 4–5 minutes. Add the mushrooms and thyme and cook over a low heat until soft. Add the brandy, cream and stock and cook gently until the mixture has reduced and thickened – about 20 minutes. Season to taste and serve with the pork.

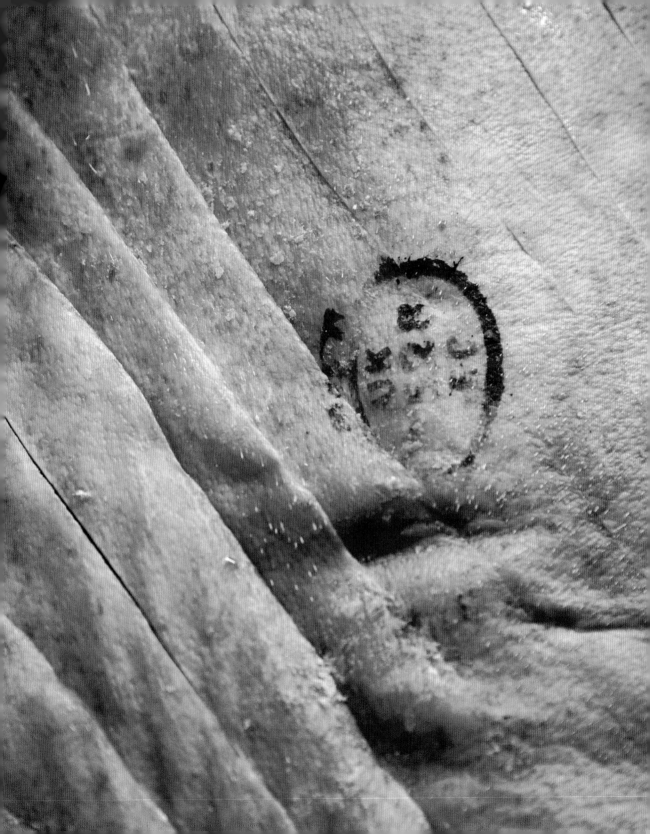

# PAN-FRIED SEA BREAM WITH CAPER SAUCE

Sea bream is an excellent table-fish. The flesh is firmly textured and cooks to white flakes. I'm used to eating it with citrus, ginger and chilli flavours, but Lee's *beurre blanc* – the other classic accompaniment – does the job magnificently.

## Serves 4

4 sea bream fillets, each about 120–140g

Flour, for coating

Salt and pepper

1 tablespoon oil

1 tablespoon butter

**For the sauce**

200ml white wine

300g butter, diced

Juice of 1 lemon

1 small bunch of dill, chopped

60g capers, chopped

Trim the bream fillets, removing any belly, and score the skin side. Lightly flour the skin side, knocking off any excess flour, and season.

Get a frying pan hot, then turn down to a moderate heat and add the oil and butter. Place the bream in the pan, skin side down, and press with a fish slice to stop the sides from curling up. Once the skin is crisp, flip the fish and cook for a further 2 minutes to finish.

For the sauce, put the wine into a saucepan and reduce by 75 per cent. Whisk the butter dice, a couple at a time, into the reduced wine over a low heat. As the cubes melt, keep adding a couple at a time until the sauce emulsifies and starts to thicken. Once all the butter is added and the sauce is thick, remove from the heat and add the lemon juice, dill and capers, then season to taste.

Serve the bream with the caper sauce poured over.

# PAN-SEARED PHEASANT WITH PARSNIP & APPLE PURÉE

It's old-fashioned to swamp game with a sticky sauce, and Lee is bang-on trend here. His purée, with bitterness and sweetness, works especially well with the pheasant.

**Serves 4**

2–4 pheasant breasts

1 tablespoon oil

1 tablespoon butter

**For the purée**

6 large parsnips, roughly chopped

5 large apples, peeled, cored and roughly chopped

500ml double cream

500ml vegetable stock

1 teaspoon grated nutmeg

Salt and freshly ground black pepper

**For the port reduction**

600ml port or cooking port

Juice and finely grated zest of 2 blood oranges

1 clove

1 star anise

To make the purée, put the parsnips and apples into a large saucepan with the double cream, vegetable stock and nutmeg. Bring to the boil and then simmer until soft and breaking down. Drain well and blitz until smooth in a food processor or blender. Season with lots of pepper and a pinch of salt to taste.

For the port reduction, add all the ingredients, except the orange zest, to a saucepan and reduce by two-thirds. Strain and add the zest.

Season the pheasant breasts and sear in a hot pan with the oil and butter for 4–6 minutes, depending on their size, then leave to rest for a further 3 minutes. The meat should still have a slight pinkness in the middle.

Serve with the purée and port reduction. Freeze any purée you don't need for up to 3 months.

# FAR EAST

## Bánh Mì II
## Cà Phê Vn

In Vietnam, life is something that happens on the street. You can get your hair cut by the barber who has set up his chair by a school, with a mirror tied to the railings; you can buy your lottery ticket at a little wooden hut by the crossroads; and, of course, you can eat. The street food in Vietnam is the best in the world. Whether it's from the woman who carries her soup kitchen in a *don ganh* (a yoke, with baskets at each end of a wooden pole) or the man who pushes a bicycle cart, and rings a little bell to announce the arrival of his fish stew, you won't be disappointed.

Pho (pronounced 'fer') is Vietnam's signature dish. The fragrant beef noodle soup is an institution. And to watch its preparation is like watching a play. First, a sieve of rice noodles is immersed into hot water, drained and poured into your bowl. That's followed by a few slices of white onion, some finely chopped chilli, a few shavings of ginger, a handful of bean sprouts and some raw beef. The final flourish is a fresh beef stock, poured over the top, and sprinkled with a grind of black pepper. You can practically eat the steam.

But the people of Vietnam are most proud of their *bánh mì* – crusty baguettes, filled with pork, homemade mayonnaise and a heavenly pâté, that are layered with crisp pickles and fresh herbs. They are sold on every street corner and, over the noise of the traffic, you can see hawkers with baskets of fresh baguettes shouting '*Bánh mì, bánh mì*'. In Vietnam, every hour is *bánh mì* hour, as long as the baguettes are still warm. When the bread lends its gentle heat to the pork, mayonnaise and pâté filling, it's something close to alchemy.

In the days of colonialism, the French would go to the deli for their filled baguettes. But when the French left Vietnam, the 'French sandwiches' (*bánh mì Tay*) went native. Because wheat had

to be imported, the Vietnamese made their baguettes with half rice flour. They replaced the duck-liver pâté with a pig- and chicken-liver pâté, they replaced the butter with a mayonnaise made from egg yolks and oil, and they replaced cornichons with a radish and carrot pickle. What started off as a pale imitation ended up as a huge improvement on the original.

Bánh Mì 11 began as a culinary venture of Ash and Van, two schoolfriends from Hanoi who couldn't satisfy their cravings for *bánh mì* in London. But now it's bigger than that – three generations are working together to bring *bánh mì* to the people. Anh and Van came up with the name because, in their mind, the perfect *bánh mì* is eleven bites big. I've never managed to make a *bánh mì* last that long, but then I'm greedy. 'It's not a simple food,' says Van. 'It's complex. And it's not just pulled off the shelf. It's cooked right in front of you.'

'It's all cooked to order,' says Anh, 'and the barbecued pork is so aromatic that you can follow the smell right up to the stall.' Then there's the baguette. The bread has to be light, so that it doesn't overpower what's inside. Which means that it has to be prooved that little bit longer. In the heat of Hanoi, that's not hard. In London? It's just that little bit harder. And freshness is all. For a baguette, one hour is considered old. Three hours, and it's dead. When Anh and Van found an East London baker who could make them fresh, warm baguettes with a thin, golden crust, and a soft, pillowy texture, they were ready. Bánh Mì 11 was born.

They made everything from scratch – even the hot chilli sauce, which is the flourish on top of a classic *bánh mì*. They roasted and shredded the pork themselves. They even pickled their own daikon, in brine, and squeezed it dry – five times. Then they set up shop in London's Broadway market. In the beginning, they put up the Bánh Mì 11 sign by climbing onto a bike seat. They 'borrowed' electricity from the laundrette next door. And they carried water from the cellar of the grocer to make their coffee. But it was worth it. The queues just get longer and longer.

Rob Atthill was planning only a brief layover in Vietnam. But he hadn't planned on meeting Tuyen, a beautiful hotel manager, in Saigon. He fell in love – with Tuyen and Vietnam. And ended up staying for three weeks. 'I adored the big boulevards, with 100ft-high plane trees that dwarfed the buildings,' he says. 'And the noise. It was absolutely crazy. People carrying whole pallets of beer, or huge sheets of glass, on the back of one motorbike. The flow of humanity was mind-boggling. I loved it. I really loved it.'

He was struck by the fact that the people of Vietnam didn't have easy access to refrigeration –

# Rob wanted to recreate a Vietnamese street café in the UK.

so they would buy blocks of ice at the market. In the heat, they still had to shop twice a day. But because the markets had such a high turnover of produce, everything was fresh. 'In the West, food can be weeks old before it gets to the shops,' says Rob. 'It's irradiated and vacuum packed. But not in Vietnam. The vegetables are fresh from the field, and the meat has been slaughtered the night before. And the street food is cooked right in front of you.'

The street is the focal point of life in Vietnam. Sitting on a plastic stool – just the right size for a small child – Rob watched the world go by. And it was worth the price of a cup of coffee for a front-row seat. Especially when it tastes like Vietnamese coffee. The thick, dark brew has an unusual caramel quality whether it's served straight up or 'cá phê sua da' – with condensed milk and ice. Rob had first heard about it from chef and food writer Anthony Bourdain. As Bourdain said in Cook's Tour, 'It kicks the shit out of Starbucks.' Rob agreed.

'If you like strong coffee,' says Rob, 'Vietnamese is the best there is. Much stronger than Italian. So I decided to import it.' But it didn't end there. Rob wanted to recreate a Vietnamese street café in the UK. 'A guy took me to the street where they manufacture only street vending carts. He took me to the street where they manufacture only little steel tables. He took me everywhere. I ended up with a container full of t-shirts, aprons, umbrellas and merchandising. I had a strong brand image straight away. If you did that in Britain, it would cost a fortune.'

The Cá Phê Vn pop-up café now travels round London's street markets in a converted ice-cream van. Mr Manfredi, who first owned the van, drove it the nine miles home from the Leyland factory. He then drove it the three miles to the market where he sold ice cream, and the three miles back again – three times a week for 31 years. Which is why the van had only 92,823 miles on the clock. All right, the clutch didn't work. It wouldn't start. And it was turquoise. But Paul Churcher, Rob's business partner, decided to buy it anyway.

'The original ice-cream chimes were still working,' says Paul. 'That's what sold it to me. They play the theme to *The Third Man*.' He was philosophical about the fact that the 1979 Leyland Sherpa had to be delivered to London on the back of a low-loader. 'I figured that we would be able to fix it. It's a classic, with the same engine as an MG. But MG people are snobby. If you ring up and say, "I need a clutch for a Sherpa," they say, "It won't fit." But if you go along with the actual clutch and just say, "I want one of them," they'll go out the back and get you one.'

To date, the Sherpa is holding up well. And it doubles as a storage unit for the metal stools, umbrellas and foldaway tables that evoke the charm of streetside cafés in Saigon. Once he's unpacked the van, Paul and Rob dish out cup after cup of Vietnamese coffee, made using the drip-filter method – which happens to go perfectly with their new range of *bánh mì*. Rob and Tuyen are slightly distracted since the birth of little Lotus. But, even on the day she was born, at 4.53am, Rob was still at the market, ready to set up, at 7am. 'Come rain or come shine,' he says.

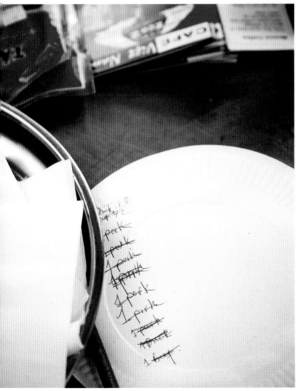

# IMPERIAL BBQ PORK BÁNH MÌ

Bánh Mì 11's Imperial BBQ Pork takes inspiration from the charcoal-grilled pork that is served with rice vermicelli and fresh herbs (*bun' cha*) on the streets of Hanoi's Old Quarter, but they make it more exciting by adding in the flavours of a marinade. The meat has a sweet taste from being caramelised but there's also a hint of shallots and spring onions. When served hot off the barbecue in a lightly toasted baguette, with carrot, mooli, cucumber and fresh coriander, it is a summer must-have for picnics, parties and family meals.

### Serves 4

| | |
|---|---|
| 4 tablespoons granulated white sugar | 4 tablespoons fish sauce |
| 100ml hot water | ½ tablespoon salt |
| 600g pork shoulder, thinly sliced | 1 tablespoon pepper |
| 2 shallots, finely chopped | 2 fresh French baguettes |
| 3 spring onions, finely chopped | Mayonnaise |
| 1 lemongrass stalk, minced (optional) | Pâté de campagne |
| 2 large garlic cloves, minced | ½ cucumber, sliced into thin slivers |
| | A few sprigs of coriander |
| | Chopped hot chilli, to taste |

Heat up a heavy-bottomed saucepan and ensure there's no water residue in it before you pour in the sugar. Stir the sugar in a circular motion, using a wooden spoon. When the sugar has turned a light brown colour, carefully pour in the hot water and cook on the stove for just 20 seconds. The key is to be swift here and err on the lightly brown side, as the sugar burns quickly and could build up enough smoke in minutes to set off your fire alarm.

In a bowl, combine the pork, shallots, spring onions, lemongrass (if using), garlic, fish sauce, salt and pepper; finally pour in the caramel sauce. Mix well and leave in the fridge for 30 minutes to marinate.

When you are almost ready to cook, thread the pork onto bamboo skewers and put on the barbecue, ideally a charcoal one to give the meat a subtle, smoky aroma.

Lightly toast the baguettes on the barbecue and then halve lengthways and spread the lower half with a thin layer of mayonnaise and pâté. Remove the grilled pork from the bamboo skewers onto the baguettes and add cucumber, coriander and some fresh chilli (if you dare). Cover with the top baguette halves, cut each one in half and you are ready to enjoy your *bánh mì*!

# CARAMELISED PORK WITH COCONUT JUICE

This is a great South Vietnamese dish, supplied by Cà Phê Vn. It needs slow cooking to make the meat tender, and is best served with steamed rice and vegetables (fresh or pickled) – with soy sauce and fresh chilli as a dip for the pork and egg.

**Serves 6**

1kg leg of pork, with fat and skin

50g brown sugar

2 tablespoons water

4 tablespoons fish sauce

2 teaspoons minced garlic

1 tablespoon salt

4 tablespoons sugar, plus extra to taste

1 fresh chilli, sliced

1 teaspoon ground black pepper

6 duck's eggs (or use hen's eggs)

1 tablespoon vegetable oil

1.5 litres coconut juice (not milk, but the clear juice from a fresh coconut)

Cut the pork into 4cm square pieces, with fat and skin, then tie them into parcels with cooking string. (This will hold them together as they cook.)

Mix the brown sugar and water in a heavy-based pan, then cook over a high heat until it caramelises. Quickly add the pork and stir well, then add the fish sauce, 1 teaspoon of the minced garlic, the salt, 4 tablespoons of the sugar, the chilli and black pepper. Cover and leave to marinate in the fridge for 2–3 hours.

Hard-boil the eggs for 10 minutes. When they are cooked, immerse them in cold water before shelling them.

Heat a little oil in a heavy saucepan or flameproof casserole and add the remaining minced garlic. When the garlic starts to brown, add the marinated pork and brown the meat. Add the coconut juice and cook for 30 minutes, before adding the shelled eggs.

Cover and cook very slowly for 3–4 hours on a very low heat or in a slow oven, until the pork is tender enough to break up with a fork or chopsticks.

Season the pork stock with salt and 1–2 tablespoons sugar, according to taste.

Before serving, remove the string from the meat. Serve hot with steamed rice and vegetables.

# CLAYPOT SHRIMPS WITH PINEAPPLE

According to Cà Phê Vn, dishes cooked slowly in clay pots are highly prized in Vietnam. It is said that the elements from the clay pots make the food special – the older the clay pot, the more delicious the food it makes. If you don't have a clay pot, you could use a small flameproof casserole. Just don't expect the same magic.

**Serves 4**

300g fresh medium shrimps or prawns, peeled

1 tablespoon fish sauce

1 teaspoon salt

1 tablespoon sugar

1 teaspoon ground black pepper

Vegetable oil

1 teaspoon minced garlic

¼ large fresh pineapple, cut into 5mm-thick pieces

100ml coconut juice (not milk, but the clear juice from a fresh coconut)

1 spring onion, sliced

Butterfly and devein the shrimps or prawns, then marinate them in the fish sauce, salt, sugar and black pepper for 30 minutes.

Heat a little oil in a clay pot or small flameproof casserole and add the garlic. When this starts to brown, add the marinated shrimps and stir. When the shrimps are beginning to cook, add the pineapple and coconut juice, and cook until the juice thickens.

Add the spring onions and a little ground black pepper and cook for a further 2 minutes.

This dish is best served hot with steamed rice.

# STEWED DUCK LEGS WITH LOTUS ROOT

This is a popular party dish in the Mekong, where duck is plentiful. It takes a while to cook, but it's worth it, as the tender duck meat and nutty lotus root make a very special flavour. Traditionally, it's also a good source of nutrition for women after childbirth. Tuyen of Cà Phê Vn swears by it.

**Serves 4**

50g dried shrimps

4 duck legs

200g lotus roots, cut into 1.5cm-thick slices

2 large carrots, cut into 4cm chunks

4 slices of fresh ginger

2 teaspoons salt

1 teaspoon sugar

1 teaspoon ground black pepper

900ml coconut juice (not milk, but the clear juice from a fresh coconut) or water

Soak the dried shrimps in hot water for 30 minutes until soft. Drain.

Heat a flameproof casserole or heavy pot and add the duck legs, lotus roots, carrots, ginger and soaked shrimps.

Add the salt, sugar, pepper and coconut juice (or water). Simmer for 4 hours (or cook slowly overnight in a slow cooker).

Before serving, remove all the fat and skin from the duck legs. Serve hot with either steamed rice or boiled egg noodles.

For extra flavour, dip the meat and vegetables into soy sauce with added chopped fresh chilli at the table.

# VIETNAMESE BEEF STEW

'This is one of my favourite breakfast dishes,' says Rob Athill, of Cá Phê Vn. 'The tenderness of the meat, the sweetness and colour of the carrots, with the fragrance of the herbs, make this a special and filling meal.' In Vietnam, this dish is often found in *pho* restaurants, served with either noodles or baguettes. It takes a long time to get the beef tender, so a pressure cooker is a good idea if you have one.

## Serves 8

4 lemongrass stalks

1 kg stewing or shin beef, cut into chunks

2 teaspoons minced garlic

1 teaspoon minced fresh ginger

2 teaspoons five-spice powder

2 teaspoons ground turmeric

2 fresh chillies, deseeded and finely chopped

2 teaspoons soy sauce

3 tablespoons fish sauce

2 tablespoons sugar, plus 4 teaspoons

1 teaspoon ground black pepper

1 tablespoon vegetable oil

1 small onion, coarsely chopped

4 whole star anise

1.5 litres coconut juice (not milk, but the clear juice from a fresh coconut)

200ml tomato juice

3 large carrots, cut into 5cm chunks

2 teaspoons salt

Rice noodles and bean sprouts, or baguettes, to serve

Chopped basil

Peel the stalks of lemongrass to get to the young flesh inside, then crush the stalks and chop finely.

Put the beef into a non-metallic bowl and mix with the lemongrass, garlic, ginger, five-spice powder, turmeric, chillies, soy sauce, fish sauce, 2 tablespoons sugar and the ground black pepper. Cover and leave to marinate for 2 hours.

Heat a large saucepan and add the oil. When it is very hot, add the onion and stir-fry until lightly browned. Now add the marinated beef and stir-fry until lightly cooked on the outside. It may take 15–20 minutes.

When the beef is lightly browned, add the star anise, coconut juice and tomato juice. Cover and cook over a low heat for 2 hours.

After 2 hours, add the carrot chunks and cook until the beef and carrots are tender.

Before serving, season the stew with the salt and 4 teaspoons sugar in order to get the correct slightly sweet and spicy flavour.

Vietnamese Beef Stew can be served with either noodles or baguettes. If you are serving it with noodles, place bean sprouts in the bottom of the bowl, add the noodles, then pour the stew in and garnish with basil. If you are serving it with baguettes, slice the bread to accompany the stew.

# COFFEE ICE CREAM

The coffee industry in Vietnam dates back to French colonialism in the 19th century. Since then the Vietnamese have made it their own, with distinctive blends and roasting styles. Very strong, high-quality espresso coffee is an everyday drink for most Vietnamese men. Condensed milk is used, because of the hot, humid climate.

This recipe from Cà Phê Vn is an ice-cream version of the famous *cá phê sua,* that retains the richness and character of the coffee.

### Makes 500ml

*397g can condensed milk, chilled for at least 3 hours*

*300ml single cream*

*60ml strong Cà Phê Vn Vietnam espresso coffee (or as near as you can get!)*

Mix all the ingredients well together, pour into an ice-cream machine and follow the instructions of the manufacturer to make your delicious coffee ice cream.

Eat immediately or pour into a plastic container and freeze for a special occasion.

# MIDDLE EAST

## Hoxton Beach

Muslims go to the mosque on Friday – it's a special day for prayer. The Hoxton Beach falafel stall, pitched up next to the mosque in London's Goodge Street, always does well on Fridays. Patrick and Rashid roll their fresh, crisp little fritters tightly into a wrap. It makes them easier to hold. 'In the Middle East you drive with one hand, and eat your falafel wrap with the other,' says Patrick – judging by the noises of approval, his customers won't be driving anywhere anytime soon…

Patrick is busy dealing with a long queue. It's the lunch-time rush. 'And I'm not as fast as the people who work for me,' he says. 'I'm certainly not as fast as Rashid and Hussein. Rashid makes wraps so quickly you can't see his hands move. But he is like: "I do not do the washing-up." Everyone wants to be a star in the falafel game, I tell you. But if you're not careful, you end up as an agent for your stars – with no business left to run.'

Wherever you go in the Middle East – whether it's Jerusalem, Gaza, Beirut or Cairo – you can find falafel. It should be a food that unites. But it isn't. Things turned nasty when the Israelis decided to make falafel their 'national snack'. The Palestinians said that falafel wasn't 'Israeli' – what with Israel only coming into existence in 1948 and all – and that falafel had originated in ancient Egypt. They felt that an Arabic dish was being stripped of its true origins.

The difficulties didn't end there. Nobody could agree on an authentic recipe for falafel. The Christian Copts – believed to be the descendents of the ancient Egyptians – make falafel with dried broad beans. But the rest of the world uses chickpeas. Or a mix of the two. 'Falafel is very diverse,' says Patrick. 'Sudanese falafel, for instance, uses dill. And it's not just about different countries – it's about different households. Some people add citrus peel. The world of falafel is very confusing.'

Patrick knows what he's talking about. He's been making falafel for years. He fell in love with it when he was studying Arabic in Syria. 'I remember feeling that this food was incredibly

healthy – all those vegetables. And incredibly delicious and cheap. I ate falafel every day. And then I got completely sick of it. Then I discovered this other thing – Syrian brain sandwich. I don't know what kind of brain it was – sheep's brain, I think – but it was very good.'

Less marketable in the UK, however, than falafel. The delicious little fritters cost pennies to make, and taste so much better than the dried-up offerings that are sold in supermarkets. And it helped that Patrick's start-up costs were tiny. 'All I needed was a fryer,' he says. 'Any kind of fryer.' Then there was the falafel maker – 'a scoop, which I picked up from an Arab shop down the Edgware Road.' And the ingredients. He was ready to make falafel.

Hackney council, however, weren't ready. In fact, they didn't want him to make falafel at all. 'But we found a legal loophole,' says Patrick. 'If you're seven metres from a road, you can trade. Someone pointed out that in Hoxton Square there was a huge car park that would be perfect.' So he set up shop in one of the coolest parts of London. He sold falafel as a late-night thing. 'People coming out of bars and clubs? Feeling rough? I thought, "Vaguely healthy food – they'll like that." And they did.'

Patrick changed the business plan along the way – what started off as 'Mandola Falafel' became 'Hoxton Beach' with the addition of a string of fairy lights and some deckchairs. But the basics – that good falafel had to be fresh, and made with the best ingredients – stayed the same. 'I remember we found ourselves in competition with a guy who was selling ready-made falafel. You're bound to do better if you make it fresh. The smells – the performance. So we took all his business. Simple.'

There are now two Hoxton Beach stalls in London. And a wholesale business, supplying health-food shops and supermarkets. Patrick

Patrick is a calm, happy man. Unless you ask him to serve your falafel in a pitta bread.

doesn't seem entirely comfortable, mass-producing food that should be hand-made. 'But if you do mechanise the process,' he says, 'you have to change the recipe to suit the needs of the machine. The mixture has got to be stiffer than if you're making it by hand, otherwise the falafel will end up like bullets. I can't have that.'

Patrick is a calm, happy man. Unless you ask him to serve your falafel in a pitta bread. 'Outrageous idea,' he says. 'And impractical. You munch your way through salad, then you get to the falafel – it's never all properly mixed. By which time the sauce will have slopped all over the place and the pitta will be coming apart. It's uncontrolled. We just use the system that is universal throughout the Middle East – the flatbread, rolled up into a wrap.'

Patrick also gets outraged at the way that, in the West, we insist on slathering hummus over our falafel. He prefers to chase each bite of crisp falafel with a drizzle of chilli sauce, and a bite of his home-made pickles; the vegetables provide a finishing blast of acid, as important to the falafel as a squeeze of lime is to *pho* and tacos. To Patrick, serving hummus with falafel is like serving chickpeas with chickpeas on the side – a bad idea. And too much for the body to digest.

Middle Eastern street food is about so much more than falafel and hummus. There are wraps of succulent grilled meat, served with tabbouleh, tomato and cucumber; and flatbread pizzas, topped with ground lamb seasoned with cumin, coriander and garlic. Men and women walk round picking at skewers of offal, and pitta breads crammed with grilled aubergine, boiled egg and mango sauce. 'We've got so much to learn from the Middle East,' says Patrick. 'But we're getting there.'

# HUMMUS BI TAHINA

# BABA GHANOUSH

The crucial thing with hummus is the quality of the tahini (sesame seed paste) – or *tahina* in Arabic; Patrick recommends al Yaman of Beirut. He also favours white Mexican chickpeas, which give a particularly creamy result.

**Makes about 20 portions**

> 500g Mexican chickpeas
>
> 175g tahini
>
> 85ml lemon juice
>
> Up to 6 garlic cloves (optional)
>
> Olive oil
>
> Salt, to taste

Soak the chickpeas overnight in a bowl of water to which a little sodium bicarbonate has been added. This makes the chickpeas softer.

Next day, boil the chickpeas in the same water until soft. Then drain, reserving some of the cooking water. Blend the chickpeas in a food processor with the other ingredients and a little reserved cooking water. Keep back some lemon juice and taste as you go for the right degree of sharpness, finally adding salt to taste. Add more cooking water if needed for the right consistency.

This is the other well-known tahini-based dip.

**Makes about 20 portions**

> 1kg aubergines
>
> 150ml tahini
>
> 100ml lemon juice
>
> 2 garlic cloves (optional)
>
> Salt, to taste

Put the aubergines over a low flame on a gas cooker or barbecue and turn them until the skin is blackened on all sides. When they are cool enough to handle, pull off the skins and discard, and squeeze out as much of the juice as you can over a sink.

Roughly blend the aubergine flesh with the other ingredients – you're looking for a rustic effect, not a smooth dip.

# FALAFEL

Key falafel fact: they are cooked by being fried – not boiled and then fried. If you try the latter, they will explode. Not good in a street food situation. Useful equipment here is a food processor; a deep fryer or a large wok; a falafel tool (*aala falafel* in Arabic) and a fryer thermometer.

**Makes about 20**

500g dried pulses made up of 175g chickpeas and 325g ful – skinned and dried broad beans, available in Turkish and Middle Eastern shops (one brand to look for is Ladin)

1 medium onion, finely chopped

1 celery stick, finely chopped

1 large garlic clove, finely chopped

White part of 1 small leek, finely chopped

1–1½ Scotch bonnet chillies, finely chopped

1 bunch of flat-leaf parsley or coriander or a mixture of the two, chopped

6g white pepper

6g ground coriander

4g ground black pepper

4g ground cumin

Salt, to taste

Oil, for deep-frying (preferably groundnut or peanut)

50g sesame seeds (optional)

1 teaspoon bicarbonate of soda

Chickpea flour (besan)

Soak the chickpeas and beans for 24 hours in a large bowl of cold water. Next day, drain them and grind them up with the vegetables, herbs, spices and salt in a food processor. You will find you have to keep scraping the sides and returning the paste for successive grinding to get it sufficiently finely chopped.

Heat the oil for deep-frying to 180°C. Stir the falafel mix in a bowl with the sesame seeds (if using) and the bicarbonate of soda.

This recipe has quite a high proportion of vegetables to beans and chickpeas. This is tasty but creates a risk: the danger is that the mixture will be too wet and need drying out in order to make a falafel ball that will hold together. This can be done by adding chickpea flour. If you start with a higher proportion of pulses – especially the broad beans, which are mushier than the chickpeas – you may well want to add water before frying to get the right consistency. When it's right it is like moderately firm mashed potato, or like saturated sand on a beach near the waterline.

Form walnut-sized balls of falafel in your hands and lower them into the fryer or wok with a slotted spoon. Carry on until the fryer or wok is full of falafel. They will rise to the surface and the bicarbonate of soda will make them puff up. Turn them with the slotted spoon and remove when golden brown; drain on kitchen paper. Eat hot, or at least warm with hummus, baba ghanoush and tabbouleh.

# TABBOULEH

Patrick isn't a fan of supermarket tabbouleh. It uses too much burghul, or bulgar wheat, to mask the fact that the parsley has been cut by machine. Any mechanical cutting pulverises the leaves, causing them to oxidise rapidly. 'Burghul is a way of hiding the evidence, like coating a murdered corpse in concrete,' he says. Cutting parsley for tabbouleh is an art: the essential points are:
1. that the parsley should be washed and completely dry beforehand;
2. that it should be held together in a bunch, so that the knife can move up it in a single action, slicing finely;
3. that it's better to put up with some oversized bits of parsley than to chop and rechop, as this will have the same bad effects as mechanical cutting.

**Makes about 20 portions**

*3 large bunches of flat-leaf parsley*

*500g firm tomatoes, chopped*

*1 small bunch of spring onions, chopped*

*1½ tablespoons dried mint*

*Salt and ground black pepper*

*3 tablespoons best-quality olive oil*

*3 tablespoons lemon juice*

*90g fine white burghul (most recipes advise pre-soaking it, but Patrick doesn't)*

Chop the parsley, following the tips on the left. Leave the stalks on while chopping, to hold the bunch together, then discard them.

Combine the parsley, tomatoes, spring onions and mint in a bowl, season with salt and pepper, then dress with olive oil and lemon juice until the salad is well coated. Finally add just enough burghul to soak up any spare liquid.

# CHURROS & PANCAKES

## Churros Garcia

## Churros Bros.

## Crêperie Nicolas

It's tough out there – on the streets. Even in the queue for a pot of churros and hot, sweet chocolate. 'We've had fisticuffs,' says Lesley McKie Garcia. 'One pregnant woman queued for an hour and a half. Someone was trying to push in. It was a Spaniard – I love the Spaniards, but they're not very good at queuing. Anyway, it ended in fisticuffs. Literally. At Churros Garcia we have to have security guards on our queues now because people are trying to bribe their way into the queue. It's ridiculous. They're only churros. But we love the effect that churros have on people.'

Lesley is churros royalty. Her mother, Encarnacion Garcia Fuenteseca, bought her first churros fryer in Madrid – the home of the churro. And when she moved to London, she brought it with her. The family stall in Petticoat Lane was the first to sell churros in the UK. 'Getting people to try them was a challenge to begin with,' says Lesley. 'Especially the men. They were too shy to take something for nothing. But the women and children would give them a go. And once they'd tried them, they loved them.'

Her dream was to take churros to London's Portobello Market. She rang up, every week, telling the market managers bad jokes down the phone until – finally – they gave in, and opened up their waiting list. 'For, literally, half a day,' says Lesley. Even then, she had to wait for four more years. But it was worth it. 'I love the fact that David Cameron used to come down every weekend. Portobello is half locals, half tourists. Perfect for churros. There are very few crossover foods. But churros is one of them – everyone likes churros.'

George Rhodes from Churros Bros wouldn't argue. He grew up on the things – his parents lived in Spain. But it wasn't until he was on holiday in the South of France, four years ago, that the crisp little fritters changed his life forever.

George bumped into a couple who were cooking their way round the coast. They went from beach to beach, wheeling the little churros machine out of the back of a van. George was trying to make a living as a documentary maker – and failing. 'So I turned to Rachel, my girlfriend, and said, "Let's quit the rat race. Let's sell churros." '

They already had the van. 'A Citroën H had come up for sale on Ebay and I thought, "I've got to have it." So I sold my decent car and bought it. Then I spent £4,000 doing it up and getting it on the road.' It was originally a butcher's van from Angoulême. 'You can still see the hooks along the back of the van where they used to hang up the meat. There's a big fridge unit at the front, to display the foie gras. And on the back we had a big butcher's block. But nowadays it's totally devoted to the pursuit of churros.'

The van causes a stir. Particularly the colours. Originally, it was a gun-metal grey. But George decided to spray it red and yellow – and the H Van anoraks never like it. 'You get a lot of guys coming up and saying, "I can't believe you've done that." I say, "What do you mean – you can't believe I've done that? You should have seen the state of it before. I've just given it another 20 years." But the whole colour scheme was based on the Selecta churros vans, which were red and yellow. So I say: "Oh, it's based on an original. Chill out." '

Finding a churros recipe wasn't quite as easy. 'No one would tell us,' says George. Lesley is typical – she won't share her recipe with anyone. 'In the markets, we're always hiding our ingredients,' she says. 'We get people with clipboards and cameras coming down every week. It's a mix of flour, water, baking powder and a pinch of sugar. I'm not shy to tell people that. But the quantities? No. Gordon Ramsay had a go on the television, and my staff phoned me up in tears of laughter because

# Let's quit the rat race. Let's sell churros.

they were uncooked in the middle. I'm keeping my recipe secret.'

To track down a recipe, George and Rachel did a couple of weeks working in churrerias in Madrid. 'In Spain,' he says, 'the churrerias open at 5am and you get this real crossover of people. There's the guys coming out of the nightclubs, and the parents and grandparents getting their kids churros for breakfast. A big mug of chocolate with churros to dip is a traditional breakfast in Spain. The churrerias crank it out all morning, and there are queues as far as you can see. I loved it – and I came away with my recipe.'

George and Lesley are agreed on the fact that good churros are all about sourcing the right flour. 'I would like to use British flour,' says George, 'but because of the climate here we just can't grow wheat with enough gluten. The only places that can are Spain, and Canada funnily enough. Canada has a really long summer. That's what gives you really strong flour. When you mix it with the hot water it forms this dough – like a bread dough. If you do that with British flour, it pours out like a Yorkshire pudding batter.'

Once the dough is made (using organic flour from Spain in the case of Churros Bros), it's fed into a *churrera* – or syringe – and extruded into a bowl of boiling hot oil. Once they are fried, the churros are then drained and served. They're not chewy. (They're chewy only if the dough is old.) They are crisp and light – like old-fashioned waffles. And there's only a pinch of sugar in the mix, so they're not sweet. Until, that is, you dip the churros into the pot of thick, warm chocolate that's traditionally served on the side.

There's as much of an art to the making of crêpes and galettes – which is why Keith and Gill Wyles of Crêperie Nicolas took themselves off to L'Ecole Maître Crêperie in Brittany to learn. With 12 others – all French natives – they learnt that galettes are made from buckwheat flour (and are better with savoury fillings) while crêpes are made from wheat flour (and are better with sweet, puddingy flavours). The pair came away with scrapers, for smoothing the batter across the griddle, and long, flat spatulas – for scraping the burnt batter off the griddle and throwing it into the bin.

Nowadays, a Crêperie Nicolas crêpe starts with the perfect batter. 'And you have to be really careful not to overwork it,' says Keith. 'If you stretch the gluten, the batter just doesn't flow.' You then have to make sure your pan or hotplate is exactly the right temperature before you pour on the batter. But you can't let the batter set into a thick puddle like a pancake. Oh no. You must swivel your wrist in a quick circular motion so that the crêpe is as delicate as possible. People with arthritis should not open a crêperie.

In many ways, crêpes are the perfect street food. They can't be made in advance, and must be created, one by one, and eaten immediately to retain their essential crêpeness. Which means that the eating must be done in the same location as the cooking. And what better location than the street? If they're folded properly, they're absurdly easy to carry. But be warned. It's origami – get it wrong, and you're left with a screwed-up bit of nothing.

Like crêpes, churros are infinitely adaptable. They were developed by Spanish shepherds, many centuries ago, and take their name from the curled horns of the Churra sheep, but there's now a world of churros out there. There's the fruit-filled Cuban churro, and the Brazilian churro that comes stuffed with *doce de leite*. In Uruguay,

coincidentally, the same place where Innocent started out. Two entrepreneurs, nervous about giving up their day jobs, had bought £500 worth of fruit and turned it into smoothies. They put up a sign saying: 'Do you think we should give up our jobs to make these smoothies?' and two bins – one saying 'YES' and one saying 'NO'. They asked people to put their empty bottles in the corresponding bin. At the end of the weekend the 'YES' bin was full – and the next day, the pair went back in to work and resigned.

The Ealing Jazz Festival was every bit as life-changing for George. He knew there was no going back, and recruited his parents to help. They drove over from Spain – with a boot full of Valor Cao. 'We've tried loads of different types of chocolate with our churros, but if the Spaniards don't get Valor Cao, they're not happy. It's rich, with a hint of vanilla, but not milky at all. It's got a really silky, thick texture that we couldn't get with anything else. The Spanish get a pot of it, and drink it on its own – the British daintily dip their churros into it, inch by inch. But everyone loves it.

'To begin with,' says George, 'Mum and Dad didn't want to help us with the festivals. They were completely against it. "Too noisy," they said.' But they helped nonetheless – at Global Gathering, a dance festival famous for its loud house, trance and dubstep. 'We sold lots of water, chewing gum and lollipops, but not many churros. We were right next to the Carl Cox tent, and after a few wines my Dad said, "I quite like this music." They have been retired for five years, but Churros Bros gave them a new lease of life.'

You can't afford to have personal-space issues if you work at Churros Bros – on a busy day, one member of the family does the frying, one does the serving and one works the dough table. 'When Dad is dough boy, you can't go near his station. And he's a Yorkshireman, so he doesn't like talking to people. You see customers trying

churros are savoury, and come filled with melted cheese. If they are thick and straight (instead of thin and curved), they're called *porras*. If they're shaped like small round doughnuts, they're called *buñuelos*. The study of churros is a life-time's work.

George's churros machine (which came from Madrid, naturally) cost 8,000 euros. But when it arrived, George couldn't get it into the van. 'I had had all these conversations about the measurements with the people in Spain, in my not-so-great Spanish, and they were like, "Yeah yeah yeah." But the machine arrived, and it was about four inches too wide. So we had to go to our local coach builder, who lives three doors down, and get an angle grinder and cut one leg off. After that, there was no going back. It had to work.'

The first public appearance of Churros Bros was at the Ealing Jazz Festival. It was,

to engage him in conversation, and he's like, "Ooh 'eck, pay over there." But we like the idea of creating a bit of theatre. That's why we got the churros machine.'

The machine requires a huge amount of electricity. So now, if a market – or festival site – doesn't allow him to plug in, George needs a generator. 'When I phone up and say I need a generator, everyone goes, "Fine," thinking I need a little compact one. I say, "No mate, I'm going to need one the size of a van". The generator I need could power a whole business park. Once I had to tow our own generator to a carnival, and people were asking if they could use some of our power. I was like, "No I need it all." They were like, "This tiny van? Are you for real? You're only making churros." '

But you live and learn. That's the nature of the business. 'One of the old school boys said, "George, you ain't got a sign on the roof mate." I said, "No, we've got this wonderful old Citroën H van. That's our sign." He said, "People won't have a clue what you're doing – your flash is your cash." I had never heard the saying. But at a festival people are pie-eyed. They've got to be able to see a sign to know what you're doing. We bought the sign, put it up and it was like, "Woah!" It just worked. People can see what we do from miles off now.

'Our biggest mistake early on was going for the big festivals, thinking, "This is obviously where the money is at – let's go in at the top." The big festivals cost a fortune – some of them are £6,500 for two days. That's a lot of fried churros. V Festival didn't work for us. People go beer, burger, band, then burger, beer, band, and they do that all day long. Womad and Big Chill are better because they're more relaxed. We're low output because everything is cooked fresh to order. But if there was a formula to all this, it would be easy.'

Churros Bros have even done Greenbelt, the Christian rock festival. 'Damn, those Christians love churros,' says George. 'Well, they don't smoke or drink, so, for them, churros and a pot of hot chocolate is as naughty as it gets.' Greenbelt was the first time Churros Bros had used social media. And they used it to good effect. The queues were huge. 'Mum was very excited, and kept saying, "Yes, everybody, I hope you read about us on Twatter." The faces of these gentle Christian folk. It was a picture.'

George loves the camaraderie of the mobilers at the festivals. They're always lending us their screwdrivers, WD40 and electric cable. 'Not the burger mafia, though,' he says. 'The "cream and greens", as they're known. They're like, "You're encroaching on our patch." It's frustrating when you see them producing awful food, and not even smiling. It's just: "Give us your money." But they're the ones driving the 4 x 4s. We see ourselves as part of the entertainment. We never close early. If you see yourself as part of the experience, you'll have a better time yourself. Just like life.'

# CHURROS

Lesley of Churros Garcia wouldn't reveal her recipe. And George took some persuading. But finally… he divulged. A recipe to make churros the way they do it at Churros Bros. Both Lesley and George serve theirs with thick Valor Cao hot chocolate.

**Makes about 24**

*250g very strong white flour (George recommends Spanish or Canadian)*

*1 teaspoon bicarbonate of soda*

*Pinch of salt*

*450ml boiling water*

*2 tablespoons olive oil*

*Vegetable oil, for deep-frying*

*Caster or icing sugar and ground cinnamon (optional), for dusting*

Put the flour, bicarbonate of soda and salt into a mixing bowl and make a well in the middle. Boil the water and mix with the olive oil, then pour into the well. Combine the ingredients together pronto, as the gluten in the flour needs the heat to get stretchy. Start by mixing with a wooden spoon. Now it's time to get involved. Get your hands in there and mix well. It's going to be hot, but worth the pain. Shape it into a sticky ball and then spoon it into a large piping bag fitted with a star-shaped nozzle. This is going to give you the familiar churros ridges that make them so crunchy.

Time for the frying. If you have a deep-fat fryer, that will be the easiest method. If not, take a heavy-bottomed pan and pour in vegetable oil till it's 7cm deep.

Heat the oil to about 185°C. Now grab the piping bag and extrude (official terminology) 10cm sticks into the oil, cutting them off with scissors. Fry a few at a time as they will swell a little, then lift them out of the oil with a slotted spoon and drain them on kitchen paper.

Sprinkle them with some caster sugar or icing sugar and cinnamon if you like. Now tuck in and think of Spain.

# CRÊPE BATTER

The perfect crêpe? The first out of the pan – a little thicker than you would have liked, maybe, and too brown at the edges. But with a sprinkle of sugar, and a squeeze of lemon, it's the cook's perk. Purists say that the perfect crêpe is the one you make once you're in your stride. When you've found your rhythm, and the pan is nice and hot. Wrong. Your first crêpe – like your first kiss – is the one that you'll remember. Here is Crêperie Nicolas's definitive recipe.

**Makes about 16**

> 500g plain flour
>
> 2 teaspoons salt
>
> 150g caster sugar
>
> 3 large eggs
>
> 900ml whole milk
>
> 25g unsalted butter, melted and caramelised
>
> 1 teaspoon vanilla extract
>
> Vegetable oil, for frying

Mix together the flour, salt and sugar in a large bowl. Whisk in the eggs and 500ml of the milk. Whisk in the butter and vanilla. Whisk in the remaining milk. Strain through a sieve (if necessary) to remove any lumps.

Cover and refrigerate for at least 1 hour before use.

Lightly oil a large, flat-based frying pan (about 37cm diameter is best), and get it really hot. Pour in a ladleful of batter and tip the pan from side to side to spread it round the base as quickly as you can. The crêpe should be as thin as possible – 50ml of batter should be sufficient for a 37cm pan. Crêpes are supposed to be very thin: they won't taste good if they are as thick as English pancakes. Each should take 20–30 seconds to cook on the first side; when the edges lift from the pan, flip the crepe over with a spatula or palette knife and cook the other side for about 10–15 seconds.

### Suggested fillings

*Butter and sugar* This is the traditional French favourite. Brush the crêpe with melted, good-quality unsalted butter and dredge with caster sugar. Fold and serve.

*Apple and cinnamon* Peel and core two Cox's apples and cut into 1cm cubes. Microwave or stew with 50g sugar and ground cinnamon to taste, until the apple is soft but still holding its shape. Spread the filling across half of each crêpe and fold first in half and then again to make a triangle shape. Dust with icing sugar and serve with crème fraîche.

# BUCKWHEAT GALETTES

Galettes are made with buckwheat which, despite its name, is unrelated to wheat. They have a delicious nutty flavour – and are deeply savoury. This is Crêperie Nicolas's recipe for galettes.

**Makes about 25 pancakes**

*500g buckwheat flour*

*15g sea salt*

*1.1 litres water*

*Vegetable oil, for frying*

In a large bowl, whisk together the flour, salt and 500ml water until completely smooth with no lumps. You can use a stick blender for this. The resulting mixture is very thick. Clean the sides of the bowl with a spatula so that the mixture is flat across the bottom of the bowl. Float 100ml water across the batter, so that air is excluded.

Refrigerate overnight, or for at least 6 hours.

Add another 500ml water and whisk until smooth. Leave the batter to rest for a minimum of 30 minutes.

Lightly oil a large frying pan (at least 37cm diameter is best), and get it really hot. Pour in a ladleful of batter – 60ml should be sufficient for a 37cm pan. Tip the pan from side to side to spread the batter round the base as quickly as you can. The galette should be as thin as possible. It should take 30–60 seconds to cook on the first side. When the edges lift from the pan, flip the galette over with a spatula or palette knife and cook the other side for about 10–15 seconds.

### Suggested fillings

*Galette complete* Turn the heat down once the galette is cooked but still in the pan, and brush with melted butter. Break an egg into the centre, so the yolk is in the middle, and spread the white around a little with a spatula. Tear a slice of ham into four and place around the yolk. Sprinkle grated cheese over the ham. Fold the edges in so that the egg yolk is at the centre and the galette is now square. Serve when the yolk is cooked but still soft.

*Cheese and spinach* Turn the heat down once the galette is cooked, and brush with a little melted butter. Sprinkle 40g grated cheese (Cheddar/Emmental/Gruyère) evenly over the galette while it's still in the pan and then scatter some baby spinach leaves over the cheese and season. Roll the pancake, and cook until the cheese is melted and the spinach wilted.

*Brie with crispy bacon and mushroom* Turn the heat down once the galette is cooked but still in the pan, and brush with a little melted butter. Place two 1cm slices of brie down the centre, scatter some sautéed mushrooms over the cheese, add four rashers of crispy streaky bacon, season and fold both sides over the filling. Cook on both sides until the cheese melts a little.

# ICE CREAM

# La Grotta Ices

On the kitchen table is a small bag of peach leaves. Kitty Travers is going to make them into a peach-leaf water ice. 'Did you know we can grow peaches in Britain?' she asks. 'Within a hundred miles of London? I think that's a bit magical. The fruit isn't amazing. It doesn't have the sun it needs. But the leaves? They taste like bitter almonds. I don't need many of them. And they're free. What's important to me is that I keep my prices down – I really want people to taste what I do.'

Everyone loves ice cream. It's the people's dessert – and Kitty wants it to stay that way. 'I love making nice little treats,' she says. 'But they've got to be nice little treats that everyone can afford. At the end of parties there are always leftovers, and I remember giving an ice cream to a homeless man – an old guy walking through Soho. He went all dreamy-eyed. He said, "I haven't tasted strawberries like that since my Mum cooked for me." That's what ice cream's all about.'

Kitty sells ice creams, sorbets and granitas at markets, festivals and private functions – but it still doesn't come easy. 'It's heartbreaking when people are walking past going: "£2.50? You can get a Mr Whippy over there for £1.50." And you're like, "But it's made of fat and air!" You might think you've got a fantastic idea – sweetcorn ice cream, for instance – but if it's not what people like, you've got to go back to the drawing board. Selling on the street is very grounding.'

The little freezer in the kitchen of her South London flat is jammed with pots of mango kulfi, milk ice cream with morello cherries, and lemon granita. 'Oh, and a raspberry and plum ice cream, flavoured with rose geranium from my Dad's balcony,' says Kitty. She shares the place with her sister, and likes to work late into the night on new recipes. 'I'm always left with a sink full of washing up,' she says. 'My sister hates me sometimes.'

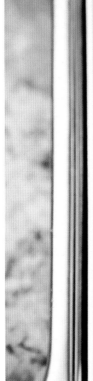

# And that summer Kitty bought a truck. La Grotta Ices was born.

She should be used to Kitty's single-mindedness by now. 'I remember when I was five or six,' she says, 'and my Mum took me and my sister to the circus. She looked round, halfway through the performance, and I was gone. She was like, "Kitty, Kitty," but I was in the litter bins, at the front of the auditorium, pulling out all the old ice-cream wrappers and giving them a good lick.' In those days it was Strawberry Mivvis. And Rockets. But a love of ice cream was always part of who Kitty was.

On the wall of the living room is a world map – and, in the corner, is a suitcase. Kitty has just got back from Iceland, where she made ice cream using only local ingredients. Which is quite an ask, in the land of puffin and whale blubber. 'Everyone was really keen to help,' she says. 'They went, "Oh yes, my grandma's got crab apples in her garden."' Kitty found angelica by the sea. And a wasteland of rhubarb near the offices of Iceland's national newspaper. The result was blissful.

Round the corner from her flat is what Kitty calls her 'shed' – a two-room Victorian warehouse, full of the trappings of her La Grotta ice cream business. Humming in the corner is a chest freezer, full of watermelon granita. And, dotted around the room, are tables and chairs salvaged from an East End café. Kitty dreams, one day, of converting the place into a tea room. It would be perfect. But, for now, the tea room will have to wait – the world needs ice cream.

Shelves run along the far wall, with everything from oyster ice-cream moulds (Kitty wants to serve ice creams, on sticks, with ice-cream pearls inside) to sundae dishes and paper napkins. Tucked out of the way are Kitty's 'fixings', such as brandy cherries, cobnuts in caramel, and quince. 'You need to keep them dark or they lose their colour,' she says. 'That's what I do in winter. I make candied fruits and marmalade – stuff I can use on ice creams in the summer. I'm like an old granny.'

Kitty started her food career in Villandry, an exquisite little foodstore on London's Marylebone High Street. It meant that she smelt of smoked eel fillets, and 80 different types of cheese (including a young pecorino imported from Sardinia). But she was happy. And she was just as happy when she worked at the London branch of the French bakery Poilâne. 'But I wasn't cooking,' says Kitty. 'I wanted something more.'

'All my friends at school were really smart, and had gone off to university. But I was stuck. I was working in sandwich shops. So when my Gran died, and left me some money, I decided to escape. Gran was a very strange eater – she used to eat cow's brains because she thought they gave her their spirituality – but she approved of travelling. So that's how I decided to use the money. I would see the world.'

Kitty had a friend who was on an academic scholarship in New York City. 'I thought, "That's what I'm going to do with my ten grand." I was kind of thinking of food. But it was more that my friend was in this really cool place, and I was stuck in London. I thought, 'I'll do a cookery course because I love cooking." Ten grand it cost. Crazy. But the course was wonderful and I didn't regret it for a second. At last I found something I was good at.'

She did the professional chef's diploma – a six-month training in everything from knife skills to sauce making. And for her three-month placement at the end of the course Kitty went to Otto, the newest restaurant opening from Mario Batali – the man they call the Don of New York. 'Everyone was like, "Why do you want to work in a pizzeria?" But ice cream was my favourite thing, and Otto had an amazing ice-cream menu.

'The head pastry chef was a scrawny, tough New Yorker – the daughter of Harvey Kurtzman, the founder of *Mad* magazine. On Monday, Wednesday and Friday she would send me down to Union Square market to pick up the Concord grapes and the maple syrup. Then I would come back and make gallons of amazing *gelato*. It was a fantasy. I had a boyfriend who was making B movies in Philadelphia, and I had never been so happy in all my life.'

After Otto, she started doing shifts in other restaurant kitchens – including Gabrielle Hamilton's Prune. 'Gabrielle liked me because I didn't have air conditioning in my apartment,' says Kitty. 'She thought that cooking was all about being strong enough to stand the heat. So she put me on fish, and made me to stand really close to the grill. My ears got really hot. I admired her, but after a while she was like, "Go back to London. London is where you ought to be. Go to St John."'

St John, that champion of British food with a carnivorous bent, was creating a real stir with its new, no-nonsense approach to food. And it had just opened a new branch – St John Bread And Wine. Even though Kitty had no formal restaurant experience, she applied for a job. 'They could see I was interested in old-fashioned English puds, and after two weeks I was given the job of deciding what went on the dessert menu. I ended up staying at St John for years.'

But she needed to go to Italy – the home of ice cream. The American Academy in Rome

was built to encourage the independent study of arts and humanities. But Kitty went there to make ice cream. 'I was living on top of a hill. In the afternoons I would cycle down to this little bar which did home-made pots of coffee and lemon granita with whipped cream for one euro. I thought, "Bloody hell – they've got it right."' Kitty had seen the future. And that summer she bought a truck. La Grotta Ices was born.

It's based in a rough part of South London, and there are metal bars on the windows. Kitty recently had her little three-wheeled ice-cream truck stolen. 'My sister went looking for it on her bike, and tracked it down to a housing estate. It was being driven about by these 13-year-old boys, who ran off, but they had caused a lot of damage.' It was nearly enough to make Kitty pull out of the British Street Food Awards – but

she made do. Her Sicilian lemon granita was voted Best in Show.

The 13-year-old boys did, however, do some lasting damage to the logo on the side of the truck. 'La Grotta means The Grotto, and the blue lips were meant to look like the mouth of a cave,' says Kitty. 'They were blue because they were cold. But I used to feel a bit embarrassed driving round town in a van with a pair of big blue lips on the side. So I won't be replacing them. Funny, really – every cloud has a silver lining.'

# LEMON GRANITA

Granita should resemble snow, sparkling with colour. And it should carry sharp flavours – like grapefruit, red wine or watermelon. 'I've had it served as breakfast, in the hot days of August, with biscotti,' says Kitty. 'And spooned onto brioche.' But the granita that won her Best in Show at the British Street Food Awards is something else. It's simple and elegant. And the best way I can think of to showcase a fresh Sicilian lemon.

## Makes I litre (serves 10)

*190ml water*

*190g golden granulated or caster sugar*

*7 large Amalfi lemons (you will need about 500ml juice)*

*150ml soda water (adds an extra tang)*

Make a sugar syrup by heating the water and sugar together in a non-corrosive pan until the sugar dissolves.

Zest the lemons directly into the warm syrup. (If there are any leaves still attached to the lemons, you can wash them and add them to warm syrup too, where they will release their rather peppery oils.)

Squeeze the lemons, strain the juice and add it to the syrup, removing the leaves if used.

Stir in the cold soda water and refrigerate the mixture for 20 minutes.

Freeze directly in a stainless-steel container – a rectangular one is best. Stir with a fork every hour or so, paying special attention to the sides of your vessel where the mix will freeze solidly if unattended. Once the mixture is firm and frozen, cover with parchment paper so that the granita is not exposed to the freezer air. Wrap in clingfilm.

To serve, place the granita in the fridge for 10–15 minutes, then scrape along the top with a heavy-duty ice-cream scoop or metal spoon (Zeroll scoops are best) to create slushy ice crystals.

Serve the granita with sweetened whipped cream (add a tablespoon of Marsala to the cream) and topping the granita with candied lemon peel.

# WATERMELON GRANITA

'Eating ripe watermelon is already like biting a slice of pink ice,' says Kitty. 'Making it into a dessert might seem like gilding the lily, but it's easily done and the result is fun and does justice to its wondrousness.' She gets watermelons imported from Sicily in July; 'so beautiful that I fall deeply in love and heave them around the house to admire the excellent colour combination in as many different lights as possible.' Thin-skinned, and heavy with juice, they crack open with the tip of a knife point, and make a thirst-quenching water ice – the natural sweetness cut through with a pinch of salt like in a good Margherita.

## Makes 1 litre (serves 10)

> 1kg watermelon flesh, cut from the rind avoiding all but the red (the leftover rinds make good pickles)
>
> Generous pinch of salt
>
> Juice of 2 limes
>
> 50g golden granulated or caster sugar
>
> 150g dark chocolate, coarsely grated (optional)

Process the watermelon flesh in a blender with the salt and lime juice. Pour the mixture though a fine sieve directly into a stainless-steel container or plastic tub suitable for the freezer. Using the back of a ladle, push it though and strain out all of the remnants of pips. Stir in the sugar, and keep stirring until it has dissolved into the juiced melon.

Place the container directly into the freezer and freeze, stirring with a fork every hour or so and paying special attention to the sides of your vessel where the mix will freeze solidly if unattended. The idea is to break up and disperse the ice crystals so that you are left with a sparkling heap of flavoured snow. Also, if not mixed well while freezing, the water will separate from the fruit, creating palomino-white patches in your granita.

Kitty likes to serve this in waxed paper cups on a hot day with straws for sucking it up when it starts to melt. She sprinkles coarsely grated dark chocolate over the top – to look like the lost watermelon pips. Or you could stud it with fresh jasmine flowers, if you happen to have any growing nearby, which is what the old ladies do in Sicily.

# ALMOND GRANITA

This is a very special water ice – and very rewarding, as you will never find anything like it commercially. This is because it is time-consuming and expensive to make. However, with inclination and relative ease you can try a true delicacy which is a rare and wonderful thing. 'Marzipan haters can do themselves a favour before going to any trouble at all and give this one a miss,' says Kitty. She uses raw organic almonds because they are cultivated from wild strains rather than grafted fruit trees and produce the odd bitter almond. As Kitty says, 'These are the magic and necessary addition which naturally contribute the essential "almond" flavour.'

**Makes 1 litre (serves 10)**

*330g unskinned raw organic almonds*

*160g golden granulated or caster sugar*

*1 unwaxed lemon*

*1.1 litres boiling water*

Grind the almonds and sugar together in a food processor for several minutes, regularly scraping down the sides until the sugar is almost dissolved, the nuts really start to warm up and release some oil and their perfume, and the whole mass becomes a homogenous paste rather than a gritty rubble. Use a rubber spatula so as not to miss anything, and transfer the contents into a large bowl. Finely grate the zest from the lemon into this mixture and quickly pour over the boiling water (heat this up in the last minutes of grinding the nuts). Combine the water with the nuts using a whisk, then cover the bowl with clingfilm and put aside for a couple of hours to infuse the flavour of the almonds into the liquid. Stir every once in a while to stop it forming a raft.

After a minimum of 2 hours, strain the mixture through a fine sieve, pressing the nut dust hard with the bottom of a ladle to extract as much 'juice' as possible. You can keep the leftover ground nuts in the freezer and replace some of the flour in cake recipes with them to add moistness or a even use them as a skin exfoliator.

Next, set up a large square of muslin or a jelly bag over a bowl and strain the mixture for a second time through this – if necessary, overnight to remove all of the solids and leave you with a milk-like almond-flavoured liquid. This is a really necessary step as otherwise your granita will be powdery and not nice at all. Add the juice of the lemon to this and proceed to freeze it as directed in the recipe on page 161.

Kitty serves this with whipped cream and cherries in brandy, but perhaps even more exceptionally delicious and easier is as a version of a Puglian speciality called *caffe in ghiacchio* – in a chilled glass with a short espresso poured over the top.

# RASPBERRY & FIG LEAF GRANITA

'Strangely,' says Kitty, 'the aroma of a fig leaf is what's often lacking from the flavour of a fig. The fruit can have sweetness, a rainy freshness and a marvellously rich texture, but sometimes misses acidity and perfume. Serving this granita with a saucer of fresh figs provides the balance, complements each separate ingredient perfectly, and creates a taste of summer.'

Kitty gets her fig leaves from a magnificent tree in London's Green Park which she first smelled one warm day in July while cycling past. 'I was 40 yards away', she says, 'but the heady scent was so strong. I'm working up the nerve to write to the Queen, asking for royal permission to use her fig leaves, hoping in the meantime that a few snapped off in the dusk of the park on a late afternoon won't be missed. But when a tree's owner is less intimidating I always ask first. The leaves seem to have most perfume in July and August.'

**Makes 1 litre (serves 10)**

*190ml water*

*190g golden granulated or caster sugar*

*375ml mineral water*

*4 freshly picked clean fig leaves, stems sliced out*

*450g raspberries*

*Juice of 2½ lemons*

Make a sugar syrup by heating the water and sugar together in a non-corrosive pan until the sugar dissolves.

Add the mineral water, bring to the boil, then toss in the fig leaves and stir them so that they are submerged in liquid. Put a lid or some clingfilm over the saucepan, turn the heat off and leave to infuse for 2 hours. Strain the liquid through a sieve and then return to the pan. Push the leaves lightly with a ladle or spatula – you want all of the syrup, but avoid squeezing the sap out of the leaves, which will be bitter.

Heat the liquid again to a bare simmer, add the raspberries, cover for 2 minutes, then turn off the heat. Give the pan a little shake and let the berries sit in the hot syrup for 10 minutes. You want to retain their fresh flavour and avoid a jammy cooked taste, but a little heat swells the fruit's cells and they give up more juice.

Purée the contents of the pan in a liquidiser with the lemon juice, then strain through a fine sieve into a stainless-steel container or suitable freezer box. Use the back of a ladle to push as much purée through as possible. The leftover pips can be added to a jug of fresh water and kept in the fridge. Strained, they make a singularly refreshing drink which keeps well for a day or two.

Freeze the granita as described in the recipe on page 161.

Serve with fresh figs or canned green figs in syrup and sweetened whipped cream. Chunks of candied orange would go well with this too.

# CHOCOLATE PUDDING ICE CREAM

This is a ridiculously simple and even low-fat ice cream which yields intense results. Sicilians used to use cornflour in *gelati* as a thickener in place of egg yolks; it's cheaper, lighter for the digestion (an Italian obsession) and it doesn't inhibit the flavours of the other ingredients like egg can.

### Makes 1 litre (serves 10)

*450ml whole milk*

*15g cornflour*

*50g best possible cocoa powder (Kitty uses Green & Black's)*

*75g golden granulated or caster sugar*

*Pinch of salt*

Mix 100ml of the milk with the cornflour to a smooth paste. Set aside.

Mix together the cocoa powder, sugar and salt in a large bowl. Heat the remaining milk to simmering, then pour in a steady stream over the cocoa mixture, whisking vigorously to prevent lumps from forming.

Return the mixture to the hob, cooking over a very low heat at barely simmering point in a stainless-steel pan. Stir the bottom of the pan constantly to prevent scorching – it can easily catch, so take care.

Cook for 6 minutes, then add the blended cornflour, whisking again to prevent lumps. Return to a simmer and cook for 2 minutes until thickened and smooth.

Strain the mixture into a clean container and cool in an ice-water bath, stirring often to prevent a skin from forming.

Refrigerate for at least 4 hours. (This 'ages' the ice cream so that the water and fat cells mingle and the ice cream has better body and melts more slowly once frozen.)

Freeze and churn in an ice-cream machine according to the manufacturer's instructions.

Serve with cashew nuts and a pinch of lightly toasted Ancho chilli seeds ground up with sea salt, or with sweetened whipped cream and grated dark chocolate.

# CHOCOLATE

## Choc Star

Petra Barran's business is flourishing. Her Choc Star brownies are on sale in delicatessens in and around London – but she doesn't want to expand. She's not just about the baking. 'If somebody wrote, "She loved baking" on my gravestone, I would be gutted. I want them to write, "She loved having adventures." I don't want to be in the kitchen – I want to be on the road.' That's where she can sell her own brand of chocolate loveliness, from the window of a converted ice-cream truck. 'That's where I have my adventures.'

She loves that truck. 'Inside, it never changes. But outside it's this conveyor belt of people from all different walks of life. From American yummy mummies in Chelsea to little kids in Middlesbrough. An old man came up to me at the Thames Festival, and said, "Can I have a chocolate ice cream, love?" I said, "That's £2." He said, "£2? For a Londoner?" I let him have it for £1.50. There's a really wonderful interplay that happens with chocolate. Nine out of 10 people smile when you say the word. It's a universally loved product.'

She drove her van round the country. 'I was ringing up town councils, saying, "I'm trying to find the most hospitable parts of Britain – can I come and park up for the day in your town and sell chocolate?" They would be like, "Of course you can." I would meet customers and say, "Can I have dinner with you?" They would look suspicious until I said, "I'll make you a chocolate pudding in return." Then they would go, "Fine. Here's the spare keys. Do you want to do some laundry?" They treated me like a VIP because I'd got chocolate.'

Petra took in the Midlands, Wales and the Peak District. But no road trip in a converted ice-cream truck would have been complete without a visit to Maryhill in Glasgow – home of the ice-cream wars. The bloody conflicts between rival ice-cream van operators took place over pitches. But Petra just parked up in the middle of town. She escaped without a tyre slashing or death threats. In fact, she ended up in a pub, dancing with old men to 'Blueberry Hill' on the karaoke. As Petra says, 'Such is the power of chocolate.'

Petra grew up around food – in an old-fashioned, Elizabeth David kind of way. Her father was a herbalist, with a rambling farmhouse in Tuscany. 'So I was raised in a big garden, basically.' The family reared pigs, made olive oil and drank rough red wine. Dinner was more likely to be tripe than truffles, and there always seemed to be

a calf's head boiling in the cauldron. 'Whenever anyone came back from holiday,' says Petra, 'the first question was always, "What did you have to eat?" That was the kind of greedy family I came from.'

The family moved to Africa. And then to England. The only thing that was expected of Petra, when she grew up, was that she would travel, and she didn't disappoint. She ended up as a stewardess on the superyachts that cruise the Mediterranean. It involved a lot of cleaning. 'But it also involved being charming to guests. Making them cocktails and serving them dinner, with a bit of supplementary flower arranging. It was the 1950s dream, really. But by the end of the evening, I always ended up hanging out in the galley with the chefs. I loved the food.'

In the Italian port of Ancona, she had an epiphany. 'I thought, "I seem to spend a lot of my time satelliting around. What should I do? Where should I go?" I was 27, and I thought, "I can't be 30 and still sleeping in a bunk bed. I've got to get off boats." But I needed a sign, so I switched on the telly. It was a Catholic church service. I thought, "Okay – it's got to be something I believe in. Something I have really have faith in. The next channel will be a sign." It was The Food Channel. And I latched on to that.'

She came back to England, thinking about a future in the food industry — PR maybe, or food journalism. She got a job working for the Black Farmer, selling his high-end sausages up and down the country. 'But it was a nightmare,' says Petra. 'And he was such an egotist.' So she thought again. And, this time, she thought chocolate. She had always loved chocolate. Growing up, people would give her chocolate cookery books – in return, she would bake them brownies. But travel had broadened her mind.

In Paris, she discovered the raspberry ganaches of Christian Constant – and his five varieties of hot chocolate. In Barcelona, she found Cacao Sampaka, the *avant-garde* chocolate shop owned by Ferran Adria's brother Albert. 'By comparison, chocolate in Britain just seemed a bit non-contemporary,' she says. 'A bit twee. So I decided to try and change people's perceptions.' A van was a good place to start. 'I didn't want to stay in one place for long anyway. So I thought, "I'll buy a van and take it round the world. Chocolate will be my social lubricant."'

While Petra looked for a van, she trained at Pierre Marcolini, a chocolatier in Kensington. She was there for six months – all the time learning. She loved Pierre Marcolini but found the staff in other high-end chocolate shops a bit stand-offish. 'Their glass cabinets were a bit of a barrier,' she says. 'And the chocolate really didn't feel that accessible. It made me realise that my van idea was absolutely right. If you inhabit the space that everyone inhabits – the street, the park – it will make your idea accessible to everyone.'

So she bought the L-reg van for £3,000 – sight unseen – on ebay. She called him Jimmy (because he was Scottish), and drove him back from Inverness to London. In retrospect, it was the wrong timing. Petra was new to the city, and hadn't had time to put down roots. 'There I was with this van – this big idea – just driving around,' she says. 'It was before I'd had Jimmy painted or anything. I was absolutely terrified. But I felt like I had to do it. I would rather do something, and regret it, than do nothing at all. It was a really stressful, stressful time.'

Petra had Jimmy sprayed by the international graffiti don Insa. Then she had him wallpapered, and fairy-lit. But her early attempts at getting him a pitch were a disaster. 'Pitches are normally allocated in advance,' she says. 'But it can get a bit heated – baseball bats and all. I got seen off a few times by belligerent Mr Whippys: "If my missus sees you here she'll be right round, and she's carrying, nowhadimean?" etc.' And when she did find a pitch, people would order tea or coffee. They weren't interested in Petra's chocolate.

But at Brick Lane market, in the East End of London, all that changed. People liked the idea of Jimmy, the van that turned up to serve chocolate that was frozen (ice cream), baked (brownies, cupcakes and flourless sponge), warmed (real hot chocolate) and iced (milkshake). 'Up until

that point,' she says, 'I was like "Is this even a good idea?" Not enough people got it. At Brick Lane everybody was saying, "This is brilliant!" Business was really good. And then lots of people started coming down. I finally found my crowd.'

Petra has the psychology of the gambler. You need it to be a mobiler. 'Every time you go out – unless it's a privately paid job – you don't know if you're going to make any money or not,' she says. 'You've got all this stock, and you hope it's going to be sunny. You hope that the people will come, that you'll be in the right spot, and that the organisers haven't overcatered it. I enjoy the question mark of it all. It's a total gamble. I think people like me get off on that. And maybe the strength of the [mobiler] community is born out of the gamble.'

It was Petra's idea to form a union. Eat Street is a collective of mobilers that gives traders bargaining power with the increasingly greedy event organisers. But it's about so much more than the money – it's about the spirit of togetherness. 'We all tend to be leaning in the rollicking-good-fun direction, with a bit of wanderlust thrown in. And we really look out for one another. Even those who seem a bit grumpsville in the beginning are soon lending you their leads/mallets/drills/milk. It's hard work, but it's a wonderful life.'

Petra craves more adventures in food. She still remembers the fish taco that she ate by the side of the road in Ensenada – 'with tequila in a plastic cup,' she says, 'and merengue wailing from an upper-storey window.' She wants to go back to the night markets in Singapore (where they served up every conceivable type of pan food), and the seafood stalls in Turkey where they sold fresh, plump mussels stuffed with a savoury rice. And there's a world of chocolate out there for her to explore. Just as long as Jimmy's clutch holds out.

# ULTRA FUDGE BROWNIES

This is the recipe for Petra's famous brownies, which she serves either on their own or on a plate with ice cream and hot choc fudge sauce cascading over them all (Brownie Fudge Sundae). It's a recipe she adapted from one of Patricia Lousada's, which she has used since she was ten. This one uses chocolate instead of cocoa, a slightly different ingredients ratio and the magic ingredient: espresso powder! Petra's grandmother used to make a Mars Bar sauce and would add coffee to give depth; the same technique does just that here.

Petra goes by the 'fudge-factor school of thought' for brownies: a glossy, almost meringue-like top, breaking easily into the deeply dense cake and with a nice swathe of satisfying fudginess at the centre. Get hold of a good, non-stick baking tin – the size of a roasting tin is perfect.

For the chocolate, Petra uses a 70 per cent Fairtrade organic blend – it's nice and fruity. In the supermarket she recommends Valrhona Guanaja if you're near a Waitrose or else Lindt 70 per cent or Green & Black's 72 per cent.

**Makes 24**

*375g dark chocolate (70 per cent)*

*250g salted butter*

*2 teaspoons instant espresso coffee powder*

*1 tablespoon cocoa powder*

*500g caster sugar*

*6 large free-range eggs*

*110g self-raising flour*

Preheat the oven to 180°C/gas mark 4. Line a 24 x 30cm baking tin or roasting dish with baking parchment.

Melt the chocolate with the butter in a heatproof bowl positioned over a pan of simmering water. When it's a good way to being melted, add the espresso powder and cocoa powder and stir until smooth.

Meanwhile, mix the sugar with the eggs in a large bowl. Give it a nice beating, preferably by hand.

Add the melted chocolate mixture and give another good stir, then sift in the flour.

Pour the mixture into the tin and bake for around 35–40 minutes, until done – not too firm, not too liquid. Set aside to cool.

These are amazing eaten warm, but brownies can taste better, and more intense, a day or so after baking.

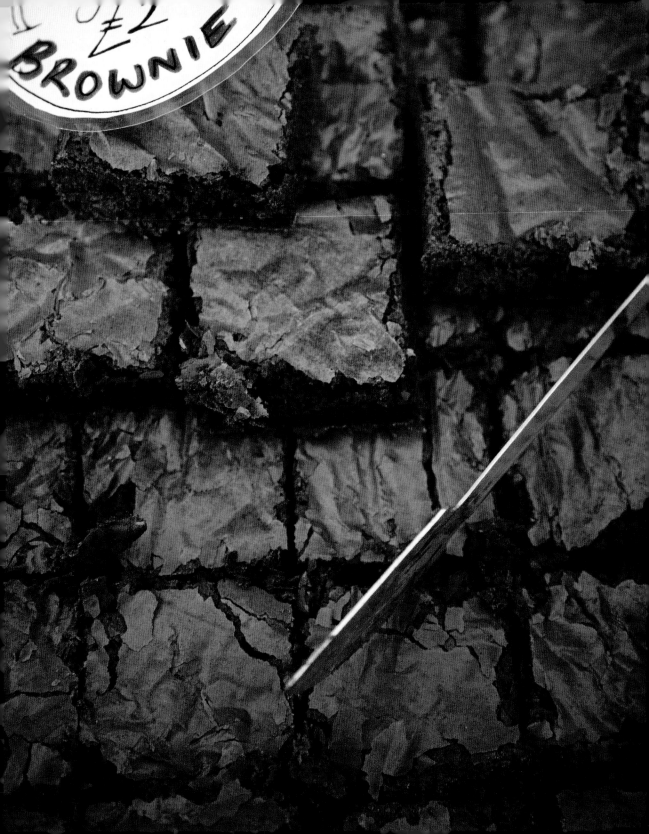

# FROZEN CHOC-DIPPED BANANAS

This is one of Petra's favourite items to serve from the van – people watcher that she is. Picture this: along comes a couple, the girlfriend chooses a banana, and Petra hands over the great chocolaty delight. 'The girlfriend looks embarrassed and starts smirking and getting to work on it,' says Petra, 'while he looks thrilled. Or mortified. Either way, we get to witness an interesting dynamic which always results in lots of laughs.'

**Makes as many as you want**

> *1 bunch of bananas (not too ripe but definitely not too green)*
>
> *Around 1 kg dark chocolate*

Line a large plastic container with baking parchment. Peel the bananas, making sure to cut off the black nodule at the end (while giving yourself a nice flat surface for future impaling). Put a short wooden skewer into the flat base of each banana (you can always use BBQ skewers and cut them into smaller sticks).

Impale with care – don't allow the stick to re-emerge elsewhere, but ensure it's in deep enough to stay put. Place the bananas in a single layer in the plastic container, cover and put in the freezer for at least 24 hours (this is so they freeze and expand to maximum capacity, so there'll be no issue with the chocolate splitting later on). If the container isn't large enough for all the bananas in a single layer, add another sheet of parchment to prevent the second layer from sticking to the first.

Next day, melt the chocolate in a large, deep heatproof bowl positioned over a pan of simmering water. Remove the bananas from the freezer and dunk into the awaiting chocolate – this may require double-dipping, depending on the depth of your choc bowl.

Lay each banana back onto the baking parchment in the container and if possible have it in the freezer as you lay them down. The chocolate should harden quickly on impact with the frozen bananas. Once all are repositioned back in the freezer with their new choc layer, cover the container and refreeze. Eat whenever you like – enjoying the hoots and smirks as people get to grips with this highly visual and interactive treat.

# CHOC STAR HOT CHOCOLATE

This is straightforward hot drinking chocolate. Or as they say in Spain, *a pelo*, which means bare-back. It's more of a bar term, but since Petra runs a chocolate bar she lets that sort of thing slide. She uses the Fairtrade organic 70 per cent blend and makes it in the van, in the Italian hot-chocolate machines that whir around in the background. This is a more domesticated version.

### Makes about 5 cups

*2 pints whole milk*

*1–2 tablespoons light brown or unrefined caster sugar, to taste*

*200g dark chocolate (70 per cent or more), broken into pieces or roughly chopped*

*Dash of double cream*

Heat the milk and sugar in a large pan until just below boiling point.

Add the chocolate and whisk it in. As the mixture becomes hotter it will emulsify and take on a silky texture. Whisk in the cream. Now for the fun bit (and she has Jamie Oliver *circa* 1999 to thank for this one): pour the hot chocolate into an empty milk container, put the lid on and, using a tea-towel to protect your hands from the heat, shake that sucker like you mean it. 'Imagine you're Tom Cruise in *Cocktail* and give it the big one' says Petra. 'When you pour that stuff out into the awaiting cups it will be velvety and fully frothed.'

### Variations
*Jamaican* Add dark rum at the end and a sprinkling of grated nutmeg.

*Hot chocolate float* Place a scoop of ice cream in the bottom of the cup, pour the hot chocolate over and then watch as it comes bombing to the top.

*Hot choc with marshmallows* Put 5–6 marshmallows in the cup, pour on the hot chocolate, and squeeze hot chocolate sauce onto the melting marshmallows.

# HI-ENERGY SUPER DARK VENEZUELAN TRUFFLES

Petra got this recipe from Willie Harcourt-Cooze in 2006 and has been using it ever since. Before Willie got his factory together and was still importing direct from Venezuela, the delivery service was much more informal – 'I remember him sending chocolate round by taxi in Prada shoe boxes,' says Petra. 'I call these truffles hi-energy because these truffles really give you a lift – even without the alcohol. It's to do with the cacao we use and it not having had the life-blood sucked out of it by endless refining. This means more of the earth-bound goodness and transcendental cacao boost.' Petra's addition is whatever good booze she has at the time. Oloroso sherry works really well, as does a nice Martinique rum.

## Makes 40

*1 x 180g bar Willie's Cacao (available at Waitrose, Selfridges or Choc Star) – the Venezuelan Black is Petra's favourite*

*150g light brown sugar*

*300ml double cream*

*A good slug of alcohol (see recipe introduction)*

*Cocoa powder, for coating*

Chop up the chocolate or power-grate in a food processor. Heat the sugar and the cream together until almost boiling; don't allow it to boil. Set aside for a few moments so that it cools from hot to warm. (Too hot and the whole lot will split and need to be resuscitated with more cream, which will dilute the power.)

Add the booze and stir through. Add the chopped chocolate and stir until it has all melted. This should result in a lovely, glossy, thick chocolate ganache. Next pour into a clingfilm-lined plastic container, pop a lid on and stick it in the fridge for a good few hours (or overnight).

Remove the set chocolate slab from the fridge, cut it into 40 cubes and form into shapes (I like to keep these pretty rustic – got a slight horror of rolling into balls). Toss in a bowl of cocoa powder and serve.

Store in the fridge, but eat at room temperature. The truffles are much more yielding and eye-rolling that way.

# CAKE

## Lulabelle's

There's something about VW camper vans. They embody the feeling of freedom in the summertime. They are cool, and symbolise 'the counterculture' – whatever that is. And they come with that 'footloose, bound-for-Glastonbury' feel fitted as standard. Which is why, for six decades, VW camper vans have been the vehicle of choice for the young – or the young at heart. It makes absolute sense that they're playing their part in the street food revolution.

The rare VW split-screen models have become increasingly collectable, and the best examples fetch over £25,000. The rarest of them all – the Barndoor Samba – can command more than £60,000. And, for the dude (or, more realistically, the hedge-fund manager) with more money than sense, there's now a company in Germany offering a VW camper with a six-cylinder Porsche 911 engine. For 150,000 euros. The waiting list is five years.

But why? VW campers are among the most impractical vehicles on the road. They stop badly and are prone to electrical failure. They weigh a ton and are underpowered. But, somehow, diehards manage to turn it all into a positive. They say that VW campers force you to drive differently – you have no choice but to slouch, and rest your elbows on the wheel. If you're in a hurry, forget it – in a VW camper, you have to watch the world fly past.

Cathy McConaghy had always loved camper vans. 'And when my daughter was born, I took her on holiday in one. For a week. It wasn't really very practical – she was only 18 months old – but I loved the vibe. Everyone was waving at us. I started buying pictures of campers. Then I got my divorce settlement through, and I thought, "Right, what am I going to spend the money on?" I started scribbling down some ideas.'

Cathy was already a successful businesswoman. 'I thought, "If I get a camper van, I've got to make it work for its money. I can't just let it sit on the drive for the odd weekends and whatnot." To begin with, I thought I could renovate it and hire it out for the hols. But then I thought, "Combine it with some catering." I always felt doing good-quality food from a camper van would work really well. It seemed like there was a real gap in the festivals market.'

'I remember going to a festival in Harrogate, where they had advertised there was an "International Food Zone." It was one caterer serving three different curries – a tiny plate of food for a tenner. It was so disappointing. When we went to see U2 in Ireland, we spent a fortune on making our own picnic. Then the security people took the lids off the wine (so we couldn't use the bottles as missiles), and drowned our food. I refused to pay for their food. So I just went to the bar. Funnily enough…'

She rang camper-van dealers all over the country. Her search took her to Bedford. 'I looked at the van, and went, "Oh my God." Not in a good way. But the more I looked at it, the more potential we could see. It was a van rather than a camper. And vans are very rare. So that meant it didn't have any windows. If it had been a camper, we would have had to take all the windows out, which would have been a shame. Within ten minutes I had fallen in love.'

VW vans were designed to be squat and powerful, and came in all sorts of varieties, including ambulances and pick-up trucks. Lulabelle was a fire engine. She was painted red, and still had all her fire equipment on board. Including the siren. But because she had spent a long time in a VW museum in Los Angeles, she was in reasonable condition. 'And she still had her original engine,' says Cathy. 'Believe it or not, she only had 23,000 miles on the clock.'

# We painted her pink and white, and we were ready to go.

Lulabelle didn't take much work to pass her MOT. Just a bit of basic bodywork. Then she went straight in for renovation. 'I chose the material for the front seat,' says Cathy. 'And fitted it. I'm all right with a staple gun and some padding. But my friend, who's a joiner, did a bit of CAD and built me a little kitchen. There's a fridge in there. And a couple of electric points for a soup kettle. But everything else is storage. We painted her pink and white, and we were ready to go.'

Cathy started off with a sandwich round, scooting round the business parks of Harrogate with her siren on. 'On the first day, I had got up at the crack of dawn to make hundreds of sandwiches,' she says. 'Hundreds. I sold five. So I had to go to the homeless with the binbags of leftovers. And even they couldn't eat them all. They said, "How long can we keep them?" I had made too many sandwiches to feed the homeless of Harrogate.'

But things got better. The customers learned to love the fact that everything from Lulabelle, down to the relish and the mayonnaise, was home-made, that day, by hand. And the packaging was biodegradable and sustainable. The sandwiches didn't taste bad either. 'So we started doing soups as well. Why not offer a decent home-made soup instead of Heinz cream of tomato? It's not hard. People started coming back for more. But it was the cakes that people loved most.'

Cathy wasn't born to bake. Not at first anyway. 'I never cooked at home,' she says. 'My first effort was for my Mum's birthday. I got some digestive biscuits, dyed them luminous green and covered them in icing.' But she got the hang of it. And, one Halloween, she found a recipe for pumpkin chocolate cake. 'There were so many different processes involved, but I enjoyed doing it. It tasted gorgeous. So every Halloween, without fail, it's a pumpkin chocolate cake. It's a tradition.'

People loved Cathy's beautiful cupcakes too, especially the chocolate chilli, the gingerbread, pumpkin and cream cheese and the sticky toffee. 'And Antony Worrall Thompson said my toffee brownie was the best he'd ever tasted.' Lulabelle was becoming more than a lunch van. And when she set up shop, it was more like high tea – with antique china plates, and matching cups and saucers. 'We became a mobile Bettys Tea Room.'

Cathy's new partner – business and pleasure – was Marcus. They met at a Halloween party, where Cathy was dressed up as herself. As a teenager. She was wearing a basque, a tutu – and pigtails. 'My head was shaved,' says Marcus, 'and I had symbols all over my head. With my mandarin jacket, I looked like an evil bouncer. It was a case of, "Will the weirdest person in the room please find the other weirdest person in the room?" So I went up to Cathy and said, "Fancy a beer?" That was it.'

Marcus was the perfect partner. For a start, he was happy in the kitchen. For the Freeze Festival, they baked 3,000 cupcakes. 'We had to work shifts,' says Marcus. 'Cathy stayed up until 3am, and then I took over. But we got there in the end.' It helped that Marcus wasn't bothered by Lulabelle's pinkness. 'I like it when this biggish,

bruiserish bloke gets out and people go, "Ah, I wasn't expecting that." She's brought out my camp side – I wear a pinny and bake muffins. I'm cool with that.'

It helps that Marcus used to rally cars to a club-car level. Which means that he knows his way round an engine – 'If it's something fairly simple,' he says. But, like most mobilers driving up and down the country, he's best friends with the AA. 'The instant the breakdown services arrive,' says Marcus, 'they have a smile on their faces. They want to help. For them, it's not just like any other recovery job. And I put all of that down to Lulabelle.'

The couple love driving along to the sound of jangling teacups and clattering saucepans. The engine is a bit noisy – Lulabelle with the pedal down sounds like a hairdresser's salon on a busy Saturday. And they know that it's not the most practical way to travel. But they like the fact that they can just stop, pull over and put the kettle on. To a couple (especially a couple from Yorkshire), that's a big part of the VW's charm.

'Every day in Lulabelle is an adventure,' says Marcus. 'When we drove to the British Street Food Awards, in Ludlow, it took us six and a half hours to get there. But it was a laugh. It's great to see people's reaction to Lulabelle if you're feeling a bit down. We have a speaker and put it on as we drive round. Mungo Jerry, Scissor Sisters – anything to make you dance. Even in Harrogate, if we're not working and the sun's shining, we drive round. People party. It's that simple.'

It doesn't bother Cathy and Marcus that there's no heating. Or power steering. Or that the windows let the air in. The couple have even got used to the fact that there's no fuel gauge. 'The only way you know how much petrol you've got left is when you run out. And it's always on a hill. Why would you want something that's cold, rattly and difficult to drive? We love it. If we had a pound for everyone who said, "We love your van, can we buy it?" we would make as much as we do on the food.'

Children are Lulabelle's biggest fans. They all point and smile and say, 'Look at the van with a face.' Cathy's daughter is no different. And she loves the Wendy House feel of the interior. 'I had it in the back of my head that when she gets a little bit older,' says Cathy, 'she can come to the festivals with us. The family ones, like Womad. She can have a little run around. The music. The bopping. She's a proper hippy chick. She will love that.'

Cathy and Marcus have big plans. In the short term, they want a commercial oven. To cut down on the shift-work that precedes every major event. In the long term, Marcus wants his own VW camper. In blue. They want to drive in convoy, park alongside each other, and compete for business. 'Cathy will have cupcakes on one side,' says Marcus. 'And I'll have boy's stuff on the other. My goat curry and chilli wraps. See which sells better.' Cathy is game. 'I can throw my cakes at you,' she says.

Until then, it's back to the lunches. And the festivals. With the odd corporate jolly along the way. 'We did one job in Yorkshire,' says Marcus, 'and Lulabelle got stuck. We couldn't get her out – it was too steep. Even in first gear. So I had to reverse, and go just fast enough to get up the hill without turning her over. It was chucking it down. And it didn't help that I had Cathy screaming in my ear. Wouldn't have got that in my old life in financial planning. But I wouldn't miss it for the world.'

# TOFFEE BROWNIES

There are hundreds of different recipes for chocolate brownies – but this one is so simple, and the addition of a really dark, heavy brown sugar gives a different dimension to the flavour. 'You really have to feel your way to success with these Toffee Brownies,' says Cathy. 'Make sure the texture gives a bit, but not too much, when you are testing whether the mixture is baked or not.'

**Makes 16 small brownies or 12 larger ones**

*350g dark chocolate, broken into pieces*

*250g butter, plus extra for greasing*

*3 large eggs*

*250g dark brown sugar (try dark muscovado)*

*85g plain flour*

*1 teaspoon baking powder*

Preheat the oven to 160°C/gas mark 3. Grease and line a 23cm square shallow cake tin.

Melt the chocolate and butter together over a low heat, then stir well and cool. Using a hand-held electric mixer, whisk the eggs until pale, then whisk in the sugar until thick, glossy and mousse-like. Gently fold in the melted chocolate mixture, then sift in the flour and baking powder and gently stir until well combined.

Pour the mixture into the prepared tin and bake for about 40–45 minutes. It needs to be firm to the touch but still have a bit of give. Keep it in the oven until you get the right feeling – not too sloppy and not too firm.

Remove from the oven and cool in the tin for at least an hour. Cut into pieces and hide in a safe place.

# CHOCOLATE PUMPKIN CAKE

When Cathy tells people about this cake, everyone says, 'I don't like pumpkin'. But they should try it first. The pumpkin content makes it really moist.

**Makes 1 x 23cm cake – about 12–15 slices**

300g self-raising flour

120g wholemeal flour

1 teaspoon baking powder

1 ½ teaspoons ground cinnamon

½ teaspoon salt

½ teaspoon grated nutmeg

½ teaspoon ground allspice

250g dark chocolate chips

200g butter, plus extra for greasing

200g dark brown sugar

6 large eggs

125g dark chocolate, melted and cooled

2 teaspoons vanilla extract

450g pumpkin purée

**For the chocolate glaze**

50g dark chocolate, broken into pieces

40g butter

40g brown sugar

3 tablespoons milk

1 ½ teaspoons cornflour

½ teaspoon vanilla extract

Preheat the oven to 160°C/gas mark 3. Grease and line a 23cm round cake tin.

In a large bowl, sift together the flours, baking powder, salt and spices. Set aside. Toss the chocolate chips with 1 tablespoon of the flour mixture and set aside.

In another large bowl, beat the butter and sugar until creamy, then add one egg at a time with 1 teaspoon of the flour so that the mixture does not curdle. Beat in the melted chocolate with the vanilla extract. Add the flour mixture and stir until thoroughly combined. Add the pumpkin purée, stir well, then add the chocolate chips.

Spoon into the prepared tin, level the surface and bake for 1 hour 20 minutes. Cool in the tin for 30 minutes, then remove and cool completely on a wire rack.

To make the glaze, melt the chocolate, butter and sugar in a small saucepan. Meanwhile, in a cup, combine the milk, cornflour and vanilla extract. Add to the chocolate and cook gently until thickened and smooth – about 1 minute. Cool for 2–3 minutes, then spoon over the top of the cake.

# GINGER CRUNCH

This traybake is a real sweet fix with a difference – and so easy to make. One of Cathy's finds from New Zealand.

**Makes 16 small or 12 larger slices**

175g butter, plus extra for greasing

175g caster sugar

300g plain flour

1 teaspoon baking powder

1 teaspoon ground ginger

For the ginger icing

50g butter

100g icing sugar

4 teaspoons golden syrup

2 teaspoons ground ginger

Preheat the oven to 190°C/gas mark 5. Grease a 23cm square shallow baking tin.

Cream together the butter and sugar until thoroughly combined. Add the sifted dry ingredients and mix well with a spoon or fork. Tip into the prepared tin and press down evenly with the back of a spoon.

Bake in the oven for 20–25 minutes until golden brown. Cool in the tin for 15–20 minutes.

To make the ginger icing, put all the ingredients in a small saucepan and heat gently over a low heat until melted and smooth. Pour over the biscuit base while it is still warm and spread out to cover the surface. Cool a little, then slice in the tin while still slightly warm.

# CATHY'S TEABREAD

No chance that we would get away without listing Cathy's teabread. In Yorkshire, a drink's too wet without it.

## Makes 1 x 900g loaf

*175g butter, melted and cooled, plus extra for greasing*

*140g clear honey*

*1 large egg, beaten*

*250g pumpkin purée*

*100g light brown sugar*

*350g self-raising flour, sifted*

*1 tablespoon ground ginger*

*2 tablespoons demerara sugar, plus extra for sprinkling*

Preheat the oven to 180°C/gas mark 4. Grease and line a 900g loaf tin.

Mix together the butter, honey and egg, then stir in the pumpkin purée. Mix in the brown sugar, sifted flour and ginger. Pour into the prepared tin, level the surface and sprinkle with 2 tablespoons demerara sugar.

Bake in the oven for 50–60 minutes until the teabread is risen and golden brown. Leave in the tin for 5–10 minutes, then turn out and cool. Sprinkle more demerara sugar over the warm cake and serve.

This tastes great spread with butter or cream cheese.

# WHOLE ORANGE CAKE

This is a bizarre recipe. But so easy. 'It's very moist,' says Cathy, 'and reminds me of hot summers.'

**Makes 1 x 22cm cake – about 8–10 slices**

2 medium, thin-skinned oranges

110g blanched almonds

220g caster sugar

1 teaspoon baking powder

6 large eggs

250g ground almonds

2 tablespoons plain flour, sifted

Icing sugar, for sprinkling

Preheat the oven to 180°C/gas mark 4. Grease and line a 22cm round cake tin.

Place the unpeeled oranges in a pan of cold water and bring to the boil. Boil, covered, for 30 minutes, then drain. Cover with fresh water and boil for about another hour. Drain and cool the oranges.

Process the blanched almonds with 2 tablespoons of the caster sugar until finely chopped.

Trim off the ends of the oranges. Cut the oranges into chunks and discard any pips. Process with the baking powder until the mixture is pulpy.

Using a hand-held electric mixer, whisk the eggs and remaining caster sugar together until pale and mousse-like. Fold in the almond mixture, ground almonds, sifted flour and orange pulp, using a large metal spoon.

Pour into the prepared tin and level the surface. Bake in the oven for 1 hour. Cool in the tin and sift with icing sugar to serve.

# CARROT & CREAM CHEESE MUFFINS

With carrots and cream cheese, these muffins are as near as dammit a health food.

**Makes 12**

280g plain flour

2 teaspoons baking powder

1 teaspoon bicarbonate of soda

½ teaspoon salt

2 teaspoons ground cinnamon

60g sultanas

1 large egg, beaten

120g light brown sugar

280g carrots, finely grated

1 teaspoon vanilla extract

2 tablespoons clear honey

90ml whole milk

90ml vegetable oil

For the topping

40g cream cheese

120g icing sugar

½ teaspoon vanilla extract

Preheat the oven to 190°C/gas mark 5. Place 12 paper muffin cases into a muffin tin.

In a large bowl, sift together the flour, baking powder, bicarbonate of soda, salt and cinnamon. Stir in the sultanas.

In a separate bowl, mix together the egg, sugar, carrots, vanilla, honey, milk and oil. Tip into the flour mixture and stir until just combined. Do not overmix.

Spoon into the muffin cases and bake for 20 minutes. Leave to cool.

To make the icing, beat together all the ingredients and pipe or spoon onto the cool muffins.

# STICKY TOFFEE MUFFINS

Years spent as a food journalist have opened my eyes to the gulf between the exquisite and the plain-bloody-awful. Take this muffin, and sit it next to a coffee chain muffin. You'll know what I mean.

**Makes 12**

200g pitted dates

250ml water

1 teaspoon bicarbonate of soda

60g unsalted butter

175g self-raising flour

175g caster sugar

1 teaspoon vanilla extract

2 large eggs, lightly beaten

**For the topping**

55g unsalted butter

70g light muscovado sugar

1 tablespoon golden syrup

100ml double cream

Preheat the oven to 180°C/gas mark 4. Place 12 paper muffin cases into a muffin tin.

Put the dates and water into a saucepan, bring to the boil, then add the bicarbonate of soda and butter. Stir to dissolve, then remove from the heat and set aside to cool slightly.

Sift the flour into a large bowl with the caster sugar, then add the vanilla and eggs.

Place the date mixture in a food processor and whiz to form a roughish paste. Add to the flour mixture and stir until just combined. Do not beat or overmix.

Pour the mixture into the muffin cases and bake for 20 minutes.

To make the topping, put the butter and brown sugar into a saucepan over a low heat with the syrup and cream. Stir to combine and simmer for 10–12 minutes until thickened. Allow to cool, then spoon over the warm muffins. For a thicker sauce, add less cream.

# COFFEE

## Caffe Banba

It's not ideal, working as a barista in a strong, southwesterly wind. The coffee pours horizontally from your portafilter. But Dominic McDermott is used to it. His pitch is on the Malin Head peninsula – the most northerly point of the Irish mainland – where the wind gusts up to 55mph. 'At that sort of speed, small children blow over,' says Dominic. 'It's not sensible to trade. But anything less than 55mph, I'll give it a go.' He parks his van cleverly – to shelter his customers – and serves them hot coffee and home-made cake. To hell with the -15°C windchill.

Round the rest of the Malin Head peninsula, coffee tastes like tea. And a 'free refill' is a threat rather than a promise. 'There was one woman,' says Dominic, 'staying at a local bed and breakfast, who had been given a cafetière – filled with instant coffee. The author of the Bridgestone restaurant guides went for a cup of coffee and the café owner reached for the Nescafe. The author said, "No thanks – have you got any real coffee?" She said, "No problem," and reached for the Gold Blend instead. No wonder he was glad to find me.'

Dominic is Malin Head's unofficial tour guide. He is forever telling his customers that Banba's Crown, the most northerly point of the peninsula, is named after the patron goddess of Ireland. And that the tower, which overlooks his pitch, was built during the Napoleonic era to keep a look-out for the French. Marconi used it in 1902 to test his state-of-the art radio equipment. Ironic really. To this day, Malin Head has no terrestrial tv. And a mobile phone signal is still treated as a magical blessing from the Lord above.

On a clear day, Dominic can see the Scottish islands. On a misty day, he can't see a thing. 'But the weather round here changes so quickly,' he says. 'It's funny, though, a bit of rain usually has quite a good effect on business. People just buy their coffee and sit in the car.' Sometimes, on a hot, sunny day, Dominic drives the Ape, his coffee wagon, down to meet the children who are swimming off the harbour. When they come out of the water, Dominic – with his hot chocolate, whipped cream and marshmallows – is the most popular man in town.

# We thought 'Why not give coffee a go?'

Dominic and his wife Andrea came to Malin Head to get their baby christened and – on a whim – bought a holiday home. As soon as they got home to England, they wanted to come back. 'So we thought, "Sod it. Let's just move."' The couple had always dreamt of running their own restaurant, but Malin Head wasn't the right place for it. So Dominic suggested a coffee cart. 'I had run the bar at university, and put in a three-group espresso machine as an experiment. It was Bradford, in 1994, but we made a fortune. So we thought, "Why not give coffee a go?"'

Dominic has always been good at dealing with the public. Back in England he had run 1970s-style discos – with a transvestite dance troupe known as the Sisters of Satisfaction and a house band called Melting Moments. 'We started it so we could play Sisters Sledge and Barry White – all on the same night.' The events were a roaring success, and regularly attracted crowds of 2,000 people. 'If we had had any business sense, we would have made a fortune.' But they didn't. Which didn't bode well for the couple's new coffee venture.

They drew up a business plan, based on extensive research of the Irish coffee market. Well, Dominic and Andrea popped up to Banba's Crown every so often to count how many people were visiting. 'We soon realised it was junk science,' says Dominic. 'We calculated that if a third of the visitors bought coffee, we would be fine. It was actually nearer a quarter. Or a fifth. Our business plan was totally irrelevant.' The couple had enough money from the sale of their house in England to keep the business running for two years – as it turned out, they needed every penny.

First, there was the van. They had bought a Vespa Ape, one of the cutest little three-wheelers on the market. 'It was a nightmare. It was brand new, but the finish was awful. I spent the first three months with my hands ripped to shreds. I had files with me at all times to file down the latest bit that had cut my hand off. And Apes are built for the Med. So up here, where it's wet and damp – and there's constantly salt in the air – it rusted away. We've had it for three years, and it's been resprayed twice. It's still covered in rust.'

The Ape wasn't the only mistake the couple made. 'In the beginning,' says Dominic, 'we ordered way too much stock. So we had boxes and boxes of crisps, and only three weeks to sell them. And postcard displays on Malin Head? Bad idea. You've got to have something that can stand up to the wind and the rain coming at you from every direction. When postcards get wet, you have to throw them away. Because I had no formal training, I was also wasting a lot of coffee and milk. We were throwing away our profits.'

But Dominic came up with an idea. 'Our coffee customers weren't after meals, but we thought they might like a slice of cake. So we bought some mini loaf cakes. But we had a look at their ingredients, and they were full of preservatives – we thought, "This isn't what we want to do. Have people come to us for really good coffee, and then send them away with manufactured rubbish." Andrea was always a good baker, and no one round here was doing anything like it. So we decided to set up a bakery. In our house.'

To start with, Dominic converted the utility

room. And one of his six toilets. But – to get the space he needed – he had to extend. 'Our baking is fairly standard. But people just don't do it any more. And we use butter. Everyone round here uses margarine.' On a busy day, Dominic now has three women working in the bakery. 'Unfortunately, our big mixer doesn't give a light enough texture to our bread and cakes. So it's all done by hand. The lemon drizzle cakes are baked in batches of three at a time. When a local shop orders 36 of them, that's a lot of work.'

He uses local flour and milk – and free-range eggs from Malin Town. 'If only I could get hold of Donegal bananas for our famous banana loaf we would be laughing.' It's not easy to introduce anything too new onto the menu. 'If people round here see an avocado, they get scared. And goat's cheese is considered exotic. Tracey, who runs a local Malin Head café called the Loaf, literally has to get her customers, sit them down, and force them to try something new. So we're breaking people in gently with our rose-water-flavoured meringue.'

The Ape is still in service. It can reach speeds of up to 40mph downhill, but you wouldn't want to hit a corner in a three-wheel Ape travelling downhill at 40mph. Especially with a one-tonne coffee machine in the back. 'So, more often than not, we tow it round. We looked at doing up an old Citroën H van, but they're a labour of love. We had two girls – then we had twins – so there was no way we would have time for a Citroën H. We went for a new Jiffy instead. Occasionally I yearn for something with a bit more character. But the Jiffy is so functional.'

It isn't fitted out with the latest in coffee technology. It wouldn't last. 'If you go to a modern coffee shop,' says Dominic, 'they will have an espresso machine that runs on 7kw electricity supplies, which we just can't do up here. Their machines cost £9,000 each, and aren't expected to drive over bumpy roads and survive. So the machine we have – the Fracino – is basic. We can't really change temperature and pressure on the road. But when we get home, we take the sides off and have a fiddle. There's very little to go wrong.'

Anyway, just because you've got a £9,000 coffee machine doesn't mean you know how to use it. There's still a lot of bad coffee out there. 'You've got people buying expensive machines,' says Dominic, 'but they don't serve the brew with any care. Dirty grinders and dirty machines – and old stale beans that stay in the grinder for weeks on end.' That's where an outfit like Caffe Banba scores highly. Dominic grinds the beans only when he needs them. The coffee is fresh. And it's served by someone who remembers just how you like it.

But he still likes to keep up with trends – the 'third wave', as it's called. It's all about the coffee. 'And not necessarily espresso coffee,' says Dominic. The Penny University (an experiment conducted by one of London's coffee roasters) didn't serve espresso at all – it served brewed coffee, made by filter, siphon and drip. And there was no milk on the counter. 'Coffee geeks deem a coffee with milk a coffee-flavoured milkshake. I find it prescriptive, telling people how they should drink their coffee. People round here like milky coffee. But I still want to give them the best coffee I can.'

Dominic knows that coffee is a delicate thing. Espresso is a colloid – a mixture of liquids, gases and finely dispersed solids. It has more than 1,500 chemical components detectable by taste and smell – far more than wine. Wine, which people get terribly uppity about, is judged to have a long 'finish' when its aftertaste lasts for over 60 seconds. The aftertaste of a good espresso lasts for 20 minutes. Even longer, if you dunk in a slice of Andrea's lemon drizzle cake.

Fíorcheann
Éireann
BANBA'S CROWN

IRELANDS MOST
NORTHERLY POINT

# THE PERFECT COFFEE

Dominic doesn't bother with an expensive coffee machine at home. Too much cleaning and maintenance. He reckons that one of the best ways to experience coffee is probably the simplest – the manual filter cone. All the equipment can be bought for less than £70. But Dominic is all about the beans, and buys from artisan roasters like Bailies Coffee in Belfast, Java Republic in Dublin, Has Bean in Stafford, and Square Mile Coffee in London. They treat roasting as an art, and go to enormous lengths to buy the best beans – in the most ethical ways possible. Dominic recommends buying single origin beans (beans of one type from a specific grower), direct from the roaster, to allow you to discover the huge variations. 'Most coffees bought in supermarkets' says Dominic, 'are blends of different types of beans, and could be roasted many months before they get to you.'

### Serves 1

*Kettle*

*Scales – Salter digital (about £15)*

*Roasted coffee beans (see notes above)*

*Grinder – Hario 'Skerton' hand grinder (about £40)*

*Filter papers (about £5 for 100)*

*Filter cone – a Hario Ceramic V60 (about £16)*

Brewing coffee using a filter cone is simple; boil the kettle. The brewing water should be somewhere between 92°C and 96°C.

Weigh the beans (30g for 500g water) and grind them. The grind should be fairly coarse, giving small granules. Grind the beans just before you brew the coffee.

Rinse the filter paper to remove the papery taste and to help it fit the cone better.

Place the filter cone with paper over your jug, place them on the scales and set them to zero. Pour in the freshly ground coffee and set the scales to zero again.

Starting in the middle and moving out in a spiralling motion, slowly pour just enough hot water (approximately 50g) to wet all the ground coffee. This should give you the bloom – the grounds will bubble and swell, and a foam will form over them.

Wait for about 20 seconds, and then slowly pour more water from the kettle until the scales show 500g. Again, pour very slowly, starting in the middle, and moving out in a spiralling motion. Try not to pour down the sides of the filter, and do not let the water pool on top of the grounds, as it will just go down the side of the cone without extracting any of the good stuff from the coffee. The brewing process should take around 2 minutes.

# BANANA BREAD

This bread is perfect on its own, but can be served with custard to make a comforting dessert. Or even toasted with butter. The recipe makes two 450g loaves, but it works even better as seven individual mini loaves if you can find cases of the right side. Make sure you use good fresh bananas – over-ripe bananas are too mushy and spoil the flavour. You can also add nuts (pecans or walnuts work well), but Dominic prefers to keep it straight up.

**Makes 2 x 450g loaves**

*250g plain flour*

*1 teaspoon salt*

*1 heaped teaspoon baking powder*

*1 teaspoon ground cinnamon*

*120g caster sugar*

*5 large bananas – not over-ripe*

*1 egg, beaten*

*75ml sunflower or good rapeseed oil*

*½ teaspoon vanilla extract*

Preheat the oven to 180°C/gas mark 4. Grease and line two 450g loaf tins.

Sift all the dry ingredients into a large mixing bowl. Add the sugar and mix thoroughly. In another bowl, mash the bananas roughly with a fork, but not too much – the look, taste and texture is far better with small chunks of banana in the baked bread. Add the egg, oil and then the vanilla extract to the dry ingredients and mix together gently. Then fold in the bananas and mix everything together, but don't overmix.

Using a big spoon, divide the mixture between the prepared loaf tins and bake in the oven for around 35–40 minutes, until the bread has risen and has a golden-brown crust. Alternatively, share between seven mini loaf cases and bake for about 20 minutes. A skewer inserted into the middle will come out clean when they are properly cooked.

# BOGGS WHEATEN BREAD

Wheaten bread is a traditional Irish brown bread made with buttermilk, giving it a moist, crumbly texture and a delicious, sweet flavour. It is so simple to make, using bicarbonate of soda as a raising agent instead of yeast. Most families in Ireland have their own wheaten recipe, but the daughter of Dominic's local butcher, Rebecca Boggs, gave him a recipe that's become legendary in the area. It is perfect served toasted, with butter, but many people simply cut off a big chunk to eat like cake with a mug of tea.

### Makes 2 x 450g loaves

*340g wholemeal flour*

*225g plain flour, plus a little extra for sprinkling*

*2 heaped teaspoons bicarbonate of soda*

*1 teaspoon salt*

*110g caster sugar*

*85g butter or margarine*

*1 egg*

*570ml buttermilk*

Preheat the oven to 180°C/gas mark 4. Grease two 450g loaf tins.

Mix together the wholemeal flour, plain flour, bicarbonate of soda, salt and sugar. Then rub in the butter or margarine until the mixture looks like breadcrumbs. Add the egg and buttermilk and mix everything together until there are no lumps – the mixture should look a bit like porridge or gruel.

Divide the mixture between the prepared tins. Sprinkle some plain flour on top, and place the tins in the oven. Bake for about 35–40 minutes until the loaves turn a lovely dark brown, or until you can stick a skewer into them and it comes out clean. Let them cool for at least 20 minutes before turning them out (a sharp tap on the side of the tin helps).

Note: If you prefer, bake one larger loaf in a 900g loaf tin. You may need to bake it for a few minutes longer.

# Index

## Recipe Credits

We would like to thank the following for giving us permission to use their recipes:

**Bánh Mì 11**, *Imperial BBQ Pork Bánh Mì* (p.120)
www.banhmi11.com

**The Bridge Inn**, *Pork Belly Stuffed with Haggis* (p.106), *Pan-fried Sea Bream with Caper Sauce* (p.109), *Pan-seared Pheasant with Parsnip and Apple Purée* (p.110)
www.bridgeinn.com

**Caffe Banba**, *The Perfect Coffee* (p.200), *Banana Bread* (p.201), *Boggs Wheaten Bread* (p.202)
www.caffebanba.com

**Cá Phê Vn**, *Caramelised Pork with Coconut Juice* (p.121), *Claypot Shrimps with Pineapple* (p.122), *Stewed Duck Legs with Lotus Root* (p.125), *Vietnamese Beef Stew* (p.126), *Coffee Ice Cream* (p.127)
www.caphevn.co.uk

**Choc Star**, *Ultra Fudge Brownies* (p.172), *Frozen Choc-dipped Bananas* (p.174), *Choc Star Hot Chocolate* (p.175), *Hi-energy Super Dark Venezuelan Truffles* (p.176)
www.chocstar.co.uk

**Churros Bros**, *Churros* (p.148)
www.churrosbros.co.uk

**Crêperie Nicolas**, *Crêpe Batter* (p.150), *Buckwheat Galettes* (p.151) www.creperie-nicolas.com

**Eat My Pies**, *Individual Pork Pies* (p.78), *Piccalilli* (p.79), *Black Pudding Scotch Eggs* (p.80), *Chicken and Ham Hock Pie* (p.83), *Custard Tart* (p.84) www.eatmypies.co.uk

**The Fish Hut**, *Perfect Fish and Chips* (p.94), *Bouillabaisse* (p.97), *Crab Cakes* (p.98), *Lobster Ravioli* (p.99)

**Greengages**, *Pumpkin soup* (p.35)
www.gogreengages.com

**Healthy Yummies**, *Scallops, Celeriac Purée, Bacon and Seashore Vegetables* (p.36), *Seared Bavette Steak with Summer Salad* (p.39), *Mackerel, Beetroot and Horseradish on Rye* (p.40), *Tomato, Lovage and Braised Celery Crostini* (p.42), *Festive Nougat* (p.43)
www.healthyyummies.com

**Hoxton Beach**, *Hummus Bi Tahina* (p.134), *Baba Ghanoush* (p.134), *Falafel* (p.136), *Tabbouleh* (p.137)
www.hoxtonbeach.com

**La Grotta Ices**, *Lemon Granita* (p.158), *Watermelon Granita* (p.161), *Almond Granita* (p.162), *Raspberry and Fig Leaf Granita* (p.163), *Chocolate Pudding Ice Cream* (p.164)
lagrottaices.tumblr.com

**Lulabelle's**, *Toffee Brownies* (p.184), *Chocolate Pumpkin Cake* (p.186), *Ginger Crunch* (p.187), *Cathy's Teabread* (p.188), *Whole Orange Cake* (p.189), *Carrot and Cream Cheese Muffins* (p.190), *Sticky Toffee Muffins* (p.193)
www.lulabelleslunches.co.uk

**The Meatwagon**, *BBQ'd Burger* (p.53), *Layover Chili* (p.54), *Meatloaf* (p.56), *The Garbage Plate* (p.57), *Dead Elvis* (p.58) www.themeatwagon.co.uk

**Rocket & Relish**, *Parmesan Chicken* (p.67), *Beef in Guinness* (p.69) *Aubergine Burger* (p.70)
www.rocketandrelish.com

**Stoats Porridge**, *Stoats Cranachan Porridge* (p.20), *Oat Crunch* (p.23) www.stoatsporridgebars.co.uk

**Street Kitchen**, *Simple Lamb Casserole* (p.66)
www.streetkitchen.co.uk